Positional
Sacrifices

Neil McDonald

EVERYMAN CHESS

First published in 1994 by Gloucester Publishers plc, (formerly Everyman Publish
plc), Northburgh House, 10 Northburgh Street, London, EC1V 0AT

Reprinted 1995

British Library Cataloguing-in-Publication Data
A catalogue record for this book is available from the British Library.

ISBN 1 85744 110 9

Distributed in North America by The Globe Pequot Press, P.O Box 480,
246 Goose Lane, Guilford, CT 06437-0480.

All other sales enquiries should be directed to Gloucester Publishers plc, Northburg
House, 10 Northburgh Street, London, EC1V 0AT
tel: 020 7253 7887 fax: 020 7490 3708
email: info@everymanchess.com
website: www.everymanchess.com

Typeset by Ken Neat, Durham

Cover Design by Brian Robins
Typset by B.B. Enterprises

Contents

1 Introduction: The Psychology of Sacrifices

It has never been more difficult to win a game of chess. Even at club level, many players have a profound knowledge of opening theory, which often reaches well into the middlegame. *Informator* is universally available, and there are now a host of specialist monographs and magazine articles. The gap between the *Encyclopaedia of Chess Openings* and the *Encyclopaedia of Chess Endings* is narrowing at an alarming rate.

So we have a problem to solve. Assuming there is no great difference in playing strength, how can we beat our equally knowledgeable and well-informed opponent in the next club game or round of the tournament?

Winning depends on at least one mistake by the opponent, and probably more. (Jon Speelman assesses it as two medium-sized mistakes before Black can expect to lose, and three for White; such is the advantage of the first move.) So the best method of play is the one most likely to make your opponent falter.

This brings us to the subject of our book: the most difficult positions to judge in chess are those with a material imbalance and dynamic chances for both sides. A sacrifice disrupts the equilibrium of the position, and can disturb and upset the opponent. This is especially true if it sets new and unexpected problems. The opponent may be in a state of shock and react in an inappropriate way. This is what Rudolf Spielmann, a Viennese grandmaster famed for his attacking prowess, meant when he remarked that a sacrifice should not be judged according to its soundness, but rather according to how dangerous it is.

Here are some examples of world-class players being bemused by a sacrifice.

Kir.Georgiev-J.Polgar
Budapest (zonal) 1993

(see diagram overleaf)

White played the spectacular 22 ♖xf7! ♔xf7 23 ♕h5+ and here of course Black played 23...♔e7 moving the king from the open file and keeping the rook on e8 defended. There followed 24 ♕xh7 ♔d8 (the bishop is indefensible) 25 ♕xg7 and Black had no good answer to the advance of the White g-pawn since her pieces are cut off from the kingside and her king is stuck in the middle. White won on move 47.

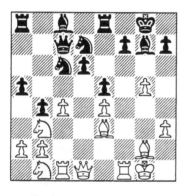

Judit Polgar is a fierce attacking player herself with a fine feel for the initiative. Therefore it is surprising at move 23 that she did not find 23...♔g8! returning the rook. Then after 24 ♕xe8+ ♘f8 25 c5 ♗b7 (as given by Georgiev) 26 ♕h5 ♘d4! Black has play for the sacrificed pawn. In any case, the game continuation is so obviously hopeless that Black would surely have chosen 23...♔g8 if she had considered it at all.

This is a clear case of sacrificial shock and stereotyped thinking. It is difficult to convince yourself that it can be correct to allow your opponent to capture a rook with check, even if

you are one of the best players in the world. It is even more difficult to think calmly and objectively when your opponent has just sacrificed a rook. One should not underestimate the demoralising effect of a sacrifice on the opponent. The following reinforces this:

Dolmatov-Lutz
Germany 1993

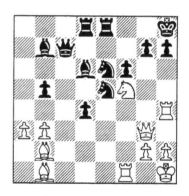

White, who has already sacrificed a knight and a pawn, continued with 29 ♖xh7+ ♔xh7 (what else?) 30 ♘e7+ g6 (30...d3 31 ♕h4 or 31 ♕h3 mate) 31 ♕h4+ ♔g7 32 ♕xf6+ ♔h6 33 ♕h4+ (a little repetition to gain time on the clock and clarify his thoughts) 33...♔g7 34 ♕f6+ ♔h6 35 ♘xg6! (D).

Now Black cannot prevent a quick mate. Note the enormous power of the bishop on b1. If 35...d3 then 36 ♘xe5+ ♔h7 37 ♕g6+ and 38 ♘f7+ wins the queen with mate to follow.

Black's pieces drop one by one as he attempts to stave off mate: 35...♗xg2+ 36 ♔xg2 ♘g4 37 ♕h4+ ♔g7 38 ♕xg4 ♘g5 39 ♕xd4+! ♗e5 40 ♕xe5+ ♖xe5 41 ♗xe5+ and Black resigned, since he is a piece and two pawns down after 41...♕xe5.

Let us return to the position after 29 ♖xh7+. Is it more natural to capture the opponent's rook than give up your queen? Maybe, but Black should nevertheless try 29...♔g8!. Then 30 ♘h6+ ♔f8 31 ♖xf6+ ♔e7! (not 31...gxf6 32 ♕g8 mate) 32 ♖xg7+ (one can sympathise with Black not wanting to have his king buffeted by white pieces, but Black has one consolation - his king has avoided the deadly power of the b1 bishop) 32...♔xf6 33 ♖xc7 ♗xc7 34 ♕h4+ ♔g7 35 ♘f5+ ♔f7. Here Dolmatov's analysis stops in *Informator 57*, with the helpful conclusion that it is unclear. The aggressive 35 ♗xd4!? also leads to equality after 35...♖xd4 (not 35...♘xd4 36 ♕g5+ with a quick

mate) 36 ♘f5+ ♔g8 37 ♘xd4 ♘xd4 38 ♕h7+ (not 38 ♕xd4? ♖d8 39 ♕g1 ♖d2) 38...♔f8 39 ♕xc7 ♖c8 40 ♕d6+ ♔f7 41 ♕xd4!? ♖c1+ 42 ♕g1 ♖xg1+ with a level endgame.

Over the board, with the clock ticking, few players would be willing to embark on such a risky adventure as 29...♔g8. Yet, as with the previous game, we can point out that the chosen continuation led to a clearly hopeless position within a couple of moves. Black had to bravely control his nerves and resist the temptation to capture the rook. A little calm objective analysis would have shown where the true chances of safety lay.

Among modern players, Alexei Shirov of Latvia is renowned for his fearless attacking play. He always seems able to turn a placid position into a dynamic fight, where material or positional deficiencies are of secondary importance compared with king safety or tactical factors. Sometimes he is punished for his gambling style, but more often than not it is his opponent who collapses under the pressure. We shall now examine some examples of Shirov's enterprising play.

Shirov-Hjartarson
Lucerne 1993

(see diagram overleaf)

There is only one open file on the

board, and although it is in White's possession, the entry points into Black's position, h7 and h8, are well defended. Black has just played 32...♘g6, attacking the rook. One imagines that White will move the rook, say to h6, when in view of the blocked nature of the position and lack of aggressive pawn advances for White, a draw seems likely. Instead White played:

33	♖xg4!	fxg4
34	♕h5	♘f8
35	♕xg4	

Black's king suddenly feels a shade draughty. The white bishop on d3 *may* strike a blow along the newly opened diagonal; the advance of the g-pawn *may* be dangerous; and the knight manoeuvre ♘g3-h5-f6 *may* be strong. Suddenly Black faces a new set of problems which have no easy solution. In time pressure, this is very disagreeable. He was probably expecting to be able to reach move 40 (the time control) with a series of nondescript

moves in a blocked position. Instead, he finds he has a lot of hard thinking ahead of him as he judges how dangerous White's threats to his king really are. Perhaps objectively he has nothing to fear, but the practical difficulties are enormous.

| 35 | ... | ♖b7! |

Black begins well enough. He brings his inactive rook to the defence of his king. But how much of Black's precious remaining time did it take to find this manoeuvre?

36	♘g3	♖f7
37	♘h5	♕b2+
38	♔f3	

| 38 | ... | ♕h2? |

In time pressure, Black not surprisingly attempts to check White's king. 'If White is in check, he cannot land a devastating blow,' thinks Black, 'and once I reach move 40, I will have time to work out just how dangerous White's threats really are.'

38...♗c3 was better, returning the bishop to active play. Then 39

♘f6+ ♗xf6 40 gxf6+ ♔h8 41 ♕h5+ ♔g8 42 ♕g4+ would draw. It is difficult to see how White can continue playing for advantage after 38...♗c3.

39 g6   ♕h1+
40 ♔f2   ♕h2+

Black has reached move 40 - but he lost on time as he did so. After 41 ♔f1 (41 ♔f3 ♕h1+ is a draw) 41...♕h1+? 42 ♗g1 ♖e7 43 ♗e4!! wins Black's queen because of the fork on f6. A better fighting chance is 41...♖e7 42 g7 (with the threat of 43 ♘f6+ queening and if 42...♘d7 43 ♗h7+!) 42...♗c3!? 43 gxf8(♕)+ ♔xf8. White must still tread carefully, e.g. 44 f5 ♕h1+ with an obscure position, but the two pieces should ultimately prove superior to the rook after 44 ♗f2.

However, Black's flag fell and that automatically finished the game. It was the problems set by 33 ♖xg4! which pushed Black over the precipice.

Shirov-Stohl
Germany 1994

A very interesting position. White's queen is attacked and if he retreats then play could continue 27 ♕d2 0-0 (27...♘xe3 28 ♕xe3 ♗f4 29 ♕f2 ♕g5 30 ♖h5!) 28 bxa6 ♖fd8. White's connected passed pawns may look impressive, but Black has very dangerous threats. The immediate one is 29...♘xe3 and 30...♗d4, and if

the white bishop moves from e3 then 29...♗f4 wins. A more aggresive non-sacrificial continuation is 27 ♕c5 when 27...♘xe3 28 ♖h5 g5!? 29 ♕xe3 ♗f4 30 ♕d4 (not 30 ♕c5 ♕xc5+ 31 ♖xc5 ♗e3+) 30...0-0! 31 ♖c5 ♕g6 32 bxa6 ♖fd8 again leaves White with menacing passed pawns, though once again his king is open to attack. Therefore, Shirov decides to sacrifice his queen in order to gain the initiative. Note that in the variations above, White's king proves a target while Black's is perfectly safe. In what follows, the situation is reversed.

27 ♕xd5!   ♗h2+
28 ♖xh2   ♕xd5
29 ♖h5!

Black must not be allowed to castle, which would safeguard his king and co-ordinate his rooks. For example, if 29 bxa6 0-0 and Black can play ...♕e5 followed by advancing his f-pawn to attack White's king.

29 ...   f5

Not a move Black wanted to play. However, he would still have been deprived of the right to castle after 29...♕e6 30 ♖c6 ♕a2 31 ♖e5+, etc.

30   bxa6

Now of course 30...0-0? loses the queen to 31 ♗c4. If 30...♕e5, White can play 31 ♗c5 (stopping castling and threatening ♗b5+) and if here 31...♔f7 then 32 ♖xf5+! ♕xf5 33 ♖f1 ♕xf1+ 34 ♔xf1 and the passed pawns and bishops defeat the two rooks. This variation demonstrates the enormous power of White's queenside pawns.

30   ...   g6

Safeguarding the f-pawn and preparing 31...h5 followed by ...♖h7. Black must get his king's rook into the game somehow, but these pawn advances weaken Black's second rank and his dark squares in general.

31   ♖h3   h5
32   ♖c7

The familiar rook on the seventh rank.

32   ...   ♖f8
33   ♗c5   ♖f7

Black has achieved his aim, but White's connected passed pawns and dominant bishops are a lethal force.

34   ♗b5+   ♔d8
35   ♖c6! *(D)*

White is not interested in exchanging rooks. The sly retreat hits the g-pawn and also introduces the idea of ♗b6+. This cannot be successfully countered

by 35...♖b8, since White simply plays 36 a4, defending the bishop, when he threatens both 37 ♖d6+ and the further advance of the a6 pawn. Black's best defence is 35...♕d1+ 36 ♔h2 ♕g4! as pointed out by Eising. Now 37 ♗b6+ ♔e7 (any other square leads to a discovered check attacking the queen) 38 ♖c7+ ♔f8 39 ♗c5+ ♔g7 40 ♗d4+ ♔f8 (forced) and it's difficult to see how White makes progress. If White plays slowly (i.e. without giving check) then Black will be able to play ...♕f4+ or ...f4-f3 starting his own attack. In any case, the game came to an abrupt end after

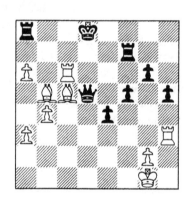

35   ...   ♖c8?
36   ♖d6+   1-0

A simple oversight, but the terrible difficulties Black has faced in this game no doubt contributed to the blunder. It is a frequently recurring theme that the psychological pressure inflicted by a sacrifice leads to a collapse later on in the game.

Connected with the theme of setting the opponent problems is that of finding the path of maximum resistance in a bad or lost position. A sacrifice can be an ideal positional trap, since the resulting positions can be irrational and hard to judge. It is easier to be 'lucky' in such a position.

Yusupov-Almasi
Altensteig 1993

White began to conquer the centre with

23   g5   ♘h5
24   e4!

The two bishops should prove significantly stronger than the black knights as the game opens up. Yusupov had foreseen that 24...♘f4 25 ♕g3 ♘d3 26 ♕xc7 ♖xc7 27 ♗xd3 cxd3 28 exd5 is winning for White. Meanwhile, White threatens 25 exd5. It seems he will acquire a protected passed pawn on d4 and the e4 square as an outpost for his pieces, e.g.

24...♕d7 25 exd5 ♕xd5 26 ♖e4 followed by 27 ♖fe1. Of course 24...dxe4? 25 fxe4 would be complete positional capitulation by Black. White would gain the f-file and a strong centre. Almasi, playing Black, is fully aware of the danger he is in. He does not fancy a slow death after 25...♕d7. So what should he do?

Black has two sources of hope in this position:

i)   White has built his centre at the cost of weakening his king's pawn cover. As long as White is in control, this weakness is irrelevant, but should Black gain the initiative, White may have cause to regret his liberal use of pawns.

ii)   White's centre is not set in steel but can be undermined by ...b5-b4.

In such positions, it is necessary to be objective - even courageous - and admit that the positional build-up has gone wrong. The only hope of safety is in counterattack and sacrifice. Therefore, Almasi played:

24   ...   b4!
25   axb4   axb4
26   cxb4

Or 26 exd5 bxc3 27 ♗xc3 ♘f4! (threatening ...♘h3+) followed by ...♘xd5 with a good game. Note that in this variation, the knight on h5 suddenly finds itself on an excellent centre square.

26   ...   ♕b6
27   ♗a4

If 27 exd5 ♘xd4 threatens

...♘xf3+. Yusupov's move forces Black to sacrifice another pawn to keep the momentum of his counterattack going.

27   ...   ♖a8

27...dxe4 28 fxe4 ♖xe4 29 ♕xf7+ ♔h7 30 ♗c2! ♕xd4+ 31 ♔h1 ♖xe1 32 ♕xg6+ ♔h8 33 ♕h7 mate is a variation that demonstrates White's attacking potential if Black is careless.

28   ♗xc6   ♕xc6
29   exd5   ♕d7
30   ♖xe7   ♕xe7

Black is now two pawns down. However, White's once proud pawn centre is in ruins. The black rook is more actively placed than its white counterpart, and is prepared to swoop down to 'seventh heaven' (...♖a2). The absence of pawns on White's second rank, save the h-pawn, means that Black's queen and rook can hope to infiltrate into the core of White's fortress through the gaps. Meanwhile, Black's king is perfectly sheltered behind his pawns. The bishop on d2 is a feeble

looking piece, and White is generally weak on the white squares. He sorely misses the bishop on d3. And because Black's pieces are so much better co-ordinated, Black's c4 pawn is much more menacing than any of White's own passed pawns. So we can conclude that Black has excellent compensation for his pawns. What prevents him from having a substantial advantage is the offside state of his knight on h5.

31   ♕e3   ♕d7!

Eyeing the h3 square. Of course, 31...♕xe3? would be a massive positional blunder. Black needs to keep the queens on if he is to generate attacking chances against White's king.

32   ♖e1   ♔h7

Black's compensation for the pawns is based on solid, permanent features of the position. So it will not disappear if he spends a move safeguarding his king.

33   ♕c3

Yusupov defends well. He sets up a blockade on the dark squares. At the same time he makes sure that the black knight on h5 doesn't get back into the game: f4 is always kept guarded.

33   ...   ♕h3

With the plan of 34...♖a2, threatening 35...♘f4! and mate on g2 whether or not the knight is captured.

34   ♖e2!   ♖a2
35   ♖f2

A notable defensive manoeuvre by White.

Has Black's attack come to an end? The bishop on d2 fends off the knight on h5; the queen on c3 keeps the rook out of a1; and the rook on f2 secures the kingside. White is now ready to push his b-pawn. Once he has assumed the initiative, he can compel Black's pieces to retreat to less aggressive squares. This would be the beginning of the end for Black. Instead, Black found a way to keep his attack going:

35   ...   ♛h4!!

You can only play deep positional chess if you are alert to tactical nuances. Without this move, all Black's fine strategical build-up would have been wasted. The queen retreats one square, leading to an almost imperceptible change in the position. Yet now there is a threat of 36...♘f4 followed by 37...♘h3+ winning, since 37 ♗xf4? is met by 37...♛xf2+ and mates. Now we see the drawback in White's apparently solid defensive line up: if any piece is dislodged, it

falls apart.

36   ♛xc4??

White's fine defensive play certainly deserved a better fate. We can surmise that White was in time trouble, and was dreaming of the initiative when he was hit by 35...♛h4!!. With only seconds to think, Yusupov snatched the c-pawn, but how should he have met the threat of 36...♘f4 here? In the cold light of study, he notes that White should play 36 ♛e3 ♜a1+ 37 ♜f1 ♜xf1+ 38 ♚xf1 ♛xh2 leading to unclear play, or 36 ♜g2 ♛h3! 37 ♜f2 ♛h4 with a draw by repetition.

However, even in his postgame analysis Yusupov is still fighting the ghost of the queen on h3. After 36 ♛e3 ♜a1+, as he suggests, White can play 37 ♚g2! and Black has no convincing way to continue his attack, e.g. 37...♘g3!? 38 ♛f4 (but not 38 d6 ♜h1! and White will be mated) 38...♘f5 39 d6 and White's passed pawn is dominant.

So Black must try 36 ♛e3 c3!? 37 ♗xc3 (37 ♛xc3 ♘f4, with the threat of ...♘h3+, is very dangerous) 37...♜xf2 38 ♛xf2 ♛xg5+ 39 ♚h1 ♛xd5. White remains a pawn up, but Black's queen and knight will co-operate splendidly to exploit White's ragged pawn structure. For example, 40 ♛f1 ♘f4 41 b5? ♛b3! 42 ♗d2 ♘d3 and White's b-pawn is lost. White's passed pawns hem in his bishop, but if he advances them they will fall victim to Black's control of the white squares. Therefore, after 40...♘f4, White would have to avoid any weakening pawn moves such as 41 b5? and limit himself to manoeuvres with the queen and bishop. A draw would then be inevitable.

The game actually came to an abrupt end:

36 ... ♖xd2!
37 ♖xd2 ♕e1+

The reader may wonder why world-class players never blunder away pieces against *them*. Well, if you can keep a top grandmaster under intense pressure during the middlegame, and then find a move like 35...♕h4!! in his time pressure, he *will* blunder.

38 ♕f1 ♕xd2
39 ♕f2 ♕xg5+
0-1

Evidently White was too short of time to resign at move 37. Here however he manages it. A great counter-attacking effort by Almasi.

It is time to summarise. To maximise our chess success, we need an 'intimidating' style that tests the calculation, imagination and endurance of our opponent. Only then will our friends marvel at our 'luck'.

2   Theoretical and Standard Sacrifices

A good combination is a sequence of moves, perhaps involving a sacrifice, that leads to an improvement in the player's position. There are no dark alleys, no obscure side variations left to chance. Everything is analysed conclusively. The player *sees the combination.*

A positional sacrifice, on the other hand, tests not only the calculating ability of the player. The player's experience and knowledge is needed to fill in the 'gaps' left by the human inability to analyse everything.

Some players have a greater capacity to calculate variations than do others. So, for example, a player such as Smyslov who has a deep feel for positional chess may play an exchange sacrifice since it 'looks right', while a Tal makes the same sacrifice only after an intense analysis of variations. Smyslov is making a positional sacrifice; Tal is playing a combination.

Of course, this is an oversimplification. Even the most positional of players calculates a huge number of variations. And every tactician makes his decisions partly based on intuition.

Kupper-Tal
Zurich 1959

Tal played 16...♘xb2 and later wrote 'in sacrificing the knight, I did not calculate variations. It would be strange if after the sacrifice, White were able to find a defence against Black's overwhelming attack' (*The Life and Games of Mikhail Tal*, RHM 1976). So not a single variation was calculated by the master tactician! How then does he know the position is overwhelming? Was he just gambling?

The game continuation proved him right: 17 ♔xb2 bxc3+ 18 ♔xc3 0-0 19 ♖b1 ♕a5+ 20 ♔d3 ♖ac8! 21 ♕f2 ♗a8! 22 ♖b3 e5 23 g5 exd4 24 ♘xd4 (24 gxf6 ♖xc2! 25 ♔xc2 ♕xa2+ 26 ♖b2 ♖c8+ wins) 24...♗xd4 and White resigned. 25 ♕xd4 ♕xe1 or 25 ♔xd4 ♖xc2 is hopeless.

No, Tal was not gambling. He did not need to calculate variations since years of experience of making sacrifices had taught him that the knight offer *must* be good. And no doubt, he had seen many similar sacrifices by other masters. The sacrifice was purely *standard*. Here is another example:

Fischer-Larsen
Portoroz 1958

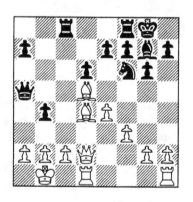

Fischer played 16 ♗b3 and remarks in *My 60 Memorable Games* (Faber 1969): 'I'd won dozens of skittle games in analo-

gous positions and had it down to a science: pry open the KR [h-] file, sac, sac ... mate!'

16...♖c7 17 h4 ♕b5 18 h5 ♖fc8 19 hxg6 hxg6 20 g4 a5 21 g5 ♘h5 22 ♖xh5! (of a similar sacrifice against Gligoric, Fischer quips 'I've played this sacrifice so often, I feel like applying for a patent!') 22...gxh5 23 g6 e5 24 gxf7+ ♔f8 25 ♗e3 d5 26 exd5 ♖xf7 27 d6 ♖f6 28 ♗g5 ♕b7 29 ♗xf6 ♗xf6 30 d7 ♖d8 31 ♕d6+ and Black resigned.

To the experienced player, sacrifices like Fischer's 22 ♖xh5! against the Dragon are so well known, even hackneyed, that it is easy to forget they were only discovered in the 1950s. Here is another common sacrifice: Black's ...♖xc3 known by all experienced Sicilian players.

Wells-Duncan
Hastings Challengers 1993/94

This game is just one of any number of similar examples.

Black played

16	...	♘xe4
17	♕e3	

This is still known theory; the experience of years of master games have taught us that Black doesn't get mated after the natural 17 ♘xe4, or rather that Black gets in first: 17...♗xd4 18 ♗xf8 ♕b6!? threatening both 19...♕xb2 mate and 19...♗e3.

17	...	♖xc3

Here it is. Black gives up the exchange to weaken White's queenside pawn structure and lay open his king to attack by Black's queen. An intuitive sacrifice? When it was first played in a similar position 40 or so years ago, yes; nowadays it is known by everyone!

18	bxc3	♘f6
19	♗xg7	♔xg7
20	♖h4	

Future generations may establish whether this position is good for White or Black, but in the present dark ages the verdict is 'unclear'. The usual theoretical moves are 20 ♘e2, 20 ♖h2 or 20 ♕e6+ according to Chris Duncan, so 20 ♖h4 may be an attempt to solve the mystery.

20	...	♖g8
21	♘e2	♗c6
22	♘f4	e5
23	g5!	♘e8
24	♘d3	f6
25	f4	fxg5
26	fxg5	♕e7

White has built up a ferocious attack, and in fact it is now mate

in 12! However, Peter Wells only had one minute left to reach the time control at move 40. As a rule, a combination is something that computers find easy, while a positional sacrifice often baffles the machine. I'm sure a computer would have found the mating sequence in one minute. But would it be able to play positional sacrifices such as 17...♖xc3?

27	♖xh7+!	♔xh7
28	♕h3+	♔g7
29	♕h6+	♔f7
30	♖f1+	♔e6
31	♕h3+	♔d5
32	♘b4+	♔c5
33	♕e3+	♔b5
34	♔b2?	

Here 34 a4+! ♔xa4 35 ♘xc6 bxc6 36 ♕e4+ ♔b5 37 ♕b4+ ♔a6 38 ♔b2! and mate by 39 ♖a1, as pointed out by Black after the game.

34	...	a6
35	a4+	♔a5
36	♔a3	♕c7
37	♖b1	♕b6

Black just survives and wins with his extra piece.

38	♕d2	♕c5
39	♔a2	♕c4+
40	♔a3	♔b6!
41	♕f2+	♕c5
42	♕f7	♖g7
	0-1	

Such standard sacrifices are discovered by the trial and error of master players. A player sees an interesting sacrifice and, after doing some analysis over the board, decides to risk it. The sacrifice proves effective, and he wins the game. Then a second player sees this game (perhaps in print, or in the flesh, or from a friend) and thinks the sacrifice looks like a good idea. He plays it at the next opportunity. And then a third and fourth player become interested...

In this process, many unsound ideas are of course eventually discarded, but others stand the test of time and become part of every player's repertory. Hence Chris Duncan can play 17...♖xc3 and know it must be quite good, whereas Alekhine could only 'risk' ...♖xc3 after a great deal of analytical work. After all, he never saw one ...♖xc3 Sicilian sacrifice in his lifetime!

The Benko Gambit 1 d4 ♘f6 2 c4 c5 3 d5 b5!? 4 cxb5 a6 5 bxa6 is well established these days as a respectable if somewhat double-edged opening system. And yet in the 1910s there was probably only one player in the world who understood the value of such a sacrifice.

Nimzowitsch-Capablanca
St Petersburg 1914

---

1 e4 e5 2 ♘f3 ♘c6 3 ♘c3 ♘f6 4 ♗b5 d6 5 d4 ♗d7 6 ♗xc6 ♗xc6 7 ♕d3 exd4 8 ♘xd4 g6

Has Black blundered a pawn? Nimzowitsch certainly thought so and eagerly played

9   ♘xc6   bxc6
10   ♕a6   ♕d7

More or less forced as 10...c5 11 ♕c6+ ♘d7 12 ♗g5 gives White a powerful attack.

11   ♕b7   ♖c8
12   ♕xa7

Now White is a pawn up and apparently has a safe position. In his book *Bobby Fischer and his Predecessors* (Bell 1976), Euwe remarks at move 8 that 'it was not so difficult to see the loss of a pawn by force in two or three moves, but Capablanca apparently did not imagine that such a thing could happen in the solid Steinitz defence of the Ruy Lopez. Capablanca's mistakes are just as clear as his good moves.'

Neither Nimzowitsch nor Euwe could comprehend that Capablanca had *deliberately* sacrificed the pawn. Euwe calls it an 'accident with a happy ending'. Capablanca himself saw things somewhat differently: 'I believe [Nimzowitsch] has been unjustly criticised for losing the game ... [the critics] have all suggested moves here and there; but the games of the great masters are not played by single moves, but must be played by connected plans of attack and defence, and these they have not given' (*My Chess Career*, Macmillan 1920). A comment that shows a deep appreciation of chess strategy.

12   ...   ♗g7
13   0-0   0-0

Black is able to improve his

position with a step-by-step plan. This could consist of the following:

i) Place the rooks on the a- and b-files.

ii) Manoeuvre the knight to c4 via g4 and e5, or perhaps d7 and e5.

iii) Win one or more of White's queenside pawns by the intense pressure of all Black's pieces. The bishop on g7 exerts enormous pressure on White's position.

Meanwhile, what should White do? He has no obvious plan, except the vague notion that he should 'defend and win with his extra pawn'. This shows one of the key features of a good positional sacrifice - it deprives the opponent of a good plan, while the sacrificer still has means to strengthen his position. The game continued:

14	♕a6	♖fe8
15	♕d3	♕e6
16	f3	♘d7
17	♗d2	♘e5
18	♕e2	♘c4
19	♖ab1	♖a8

Black's plan gradually unfolds while White flounders.

| 20 | a4 | ♘xd2! |

Removing the one piece that could challenge the supremacy of Black's dominant g7 bishop.

| 21 | ♕xd2 | ♕c4 |
| 22 | ♖fd1 | ♖eb8 |

Black's pieces are now beautifully co-ordinated. Every piece contributes to the plan of attack

on the queenside and White doesn't have a ghost of counterplay.

| 23 | ♕e3 | ♖b4 |
| 24 | ♕g5 | |

All White can do is respond to one move threats. There is no harmony among his pieces.

| 24 | ... | ♗d4+ |
| 25 | ♔h1 | ♖ab8 |

The pressure intensifies. Now White has no choice but to sacrifice the exchange, since 26...♗xc3 is threatened and the knight has no good moves.

| 26 | ♖xd4 | ♕xd4 |
| 27 | ♖d1 | ♕c4 |

Now b2 is dropping and White's game collapses. The final moves were: **28 h4 ♖xb2 29 ♕d2 ♕c5 30 ♖e1 ♕h5 31 ♖a1 ♕xh4+ 32 ♔g1 ♕h5 33 a5 ♖a8 34 a6 ♕c5+ 25 ♔h1 ♕c4 36 a7 ♕c5 0-1**

This game, one of Capablanca's best, is not included in Golombek's book *Capablanca's 100 Best Games*. Like Euwe and Nimzowitsch, Golombek, it seems, believed Capablanca had simply blundered a pawn! Almost any strong *modern* player would appreciate the value of Capablanca's concept. Why then were Euwe and Nimzowitsch, two of the strongest players in the history of chess, blind to the merits of the sacrifice? The answer is that they had never seen such a concept before. They had no internal model against which to judge the sacrifice. Therefore it was easy to believe that the pawn offer was simply a blunder. But the question remains: if Euwe and Nimzowitsch could not understand the sacrifice, how could Capablanca conceive it? Well, Capablanca was a genius!

There are also many standard sacrificial ideas in the endgame. We shall look at several interesting examples.

Black cannot win, since White's rook oscillates between e3 and g3 where it is defended by the f2 pawn. Meanwhile, the white king cannot be driven from the g1 or g2 square where it defends the f2 pawn. Black's king cannot approach, so the game is drawn.

Note that this is White's ideal defensive set up. A slight change could spell defeat. For example, put White's king on e1. Now if White can get his king to g1, we have the book draw above. However, 1 ♔f1 ♕h1+ frustrates him. Then 2 ♔e2 ♔h4 3 ♖g3 ♕c1 4 ♖e3 ♕b1! 5 ♖g3 (5 ♖d3 ♕b2+ 6

♔f1 ♕b1+ 7 ♔e2 ♕c2+ 8 ♖d2 ♕e4+ and 9...g3 exchanges pawns, thereby breaking the blockade, as does 5 ♔d2 ♕f1 6 ♖e2 g3) 5...♕b5+ 6 ♔e1 ♕e5+ 7 ♖e3 (7 ♔f1 ♕xg3! 8 fxg3+ ♔xg3 9 ♔g1 ♔h3 10 ♔h1 g3 and wins) 7...♕xe3+! 8 fxe3 ♔h3 and the king shepherds home the passed pawn long before White's own pawn gets moving.

A knowledge of such blockades can save a lot of heartache. I remember Kupreichik, the Russian grandmaster, giving a simultaneous exhibition against the top British juniors some years ago. In one game his opponent had an easily winning position, a piece up for nothing, but unfortunately he followed a well-known piece of advice if you are material up: exchange off at every opportunity. One by one the pieces disappeared, then Kupreichik 'blundered' his queen ... and finally reached a drawn position very similar to the diagram above. Here is another example:

Kir.Georgiev-Anand
Las Palmas 1993

(see following diagram)

Things look desperate for Black, since he must lose a piece. But remembering our blockade above, 32...♖g2!? suggests itself. Then 33 ♕xe3 ♖xe2 34 ♕xe2 a6! (ruling out any disruptive a6 by White) and White cannot win.

Even if White wins the e5 and h7 pawns, Black could establish a blockade like the following:

(analysis diagram)

The black rook swings from b5 to d5 and back again. When the rook is on d5, the sacrifice ♕xd5+ cxd5, ♔xd5 is only a draw. But in the game, Anand tried

32   ...   ♖g4

Perhaps he was playing for a win?

33   a6!

33 ♕xe3 ♖a4+ 34 ♔b3 ♖xa5

leads to a curious material balance. There are no weaknesses in Black's position and he can hardly lose. Neither has he any winning tries, so a draw would be inevitable.

33   ...   ♖a4+

Black would have to resign after 33...♖e4? or 33...b6? 34 ♕f7!.

34   ♔b3   ♖xa6
35   ♗xa6

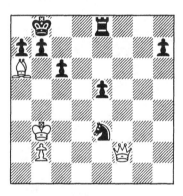

35   ...   ♘d5!

If 35...bxa6? 36 ♕xe3 and Black wouldn't be able to set up a blockade, e.g. 36...♔b7 37 ♕d3 ♔b6 38 ♔c4 ♖g8 39 ♕e3+ ♔b7 40 ♕xe5 ♖c8 41 ♔c5 ♖c7 42 ♔d6 and wins, or 36...♖d8 37 ♕xe5+ ♔c8 38 ♕c5 ♔b7 39 ♕e7+ ♔b8 40 ♕xa7 ♖d5 41 ♕xa6+ ♔c7. With the black pawn on the third rank rather than the second, the blockade fails, e.g. 42 ♕a7+ ♔c8 43 ♕xh7 ♖b5+ 44 ♔c4 ♔b8 (44...♖xb2 loses the rook after 45 ♕g8+, etc.) 45 b4 ♖d5 46 ♕f7 (threatening 47 ♕xd5) 46...♖b5

47 ♕d7 and the blockade crumbles after 47...♖b6 48 ♔c5. Note that there is no blockade draw with a rook's pawn:

(analysis diagram)

This is because the rook's pawn only produces one safe square for the rook, not two. So in the diagram position, Black loses after 1 ♕d7! and the rook has no safe move: 1...♖h6 2 ♕e8+ ♔b7 3 ♕e4+ ♖c6+ (everything else loses the rook to a check, e.g. 4...♔c7 5 ♕f4+ ♖d6 6 ♔c5) 4 ♔b5 a6+ 5 ♔a5 ♔c7 6 ♕xc6+! ♔xc6 7 ♔xa6 and wins. Hence, Anand was right to play 35...♘d5!. We return to his game.

36	♗c4	e4
37	♕f7	♖d8
38	♕xh7	e3
39	♕h2+	♔a8
40	♕e5	a6
41	♕e4	♖f8
42	♗xd5	

Georgiev realises there is no way to progress without this exchange. But now we reach a clearly drawn blockade position.

42	...	cxd5
43	♕xe3	♖c8
44	♕e6	♖c6

44...♖c5 would allow White to weaken the blockade after 45 ♕e8+ ♔a7 46 ♕e3 b6 47 ♕e7+ ♔b8 48 ♔a2!? with the idea of b2-b4 undermining the rook. 44...♖c6 is simpler.

45	♕xd5	♖b6+
46	♔a3	♖b5
47	♕d4	♔b8
48	b3	♔a8
49	♔b2	♔b8
50	♔c3	♔a8
51	♔c4	♔b8
52	b4	♔c7?!

As Anand points out, 52...♔a8 is more accurate with a total draw.

| 53 | ♕f4+! | |

A cunning move, hoping for 53...♔c8 34 ♕d6! when Black loses since he is in zugzwang, e.g. 54...b6 55 ♕e7 ♔b8 (or 56 ♕a7 wins) 56 ♕d7 ♔a8 57 ♕c7 and wins.

| 53 | ... | ♔b6! |

But this is good enough to draw.

54	♕b8	♖h5
55	♔b3	♖b5
56	♔a4	♖d5

and a draw was agreed.

Pinter-Kasparov
France 1993

(see following diagram)
Kasparov is evidently on the brink of defeat. But like all world

champions, he has an intense will to survive. Therefore it is not surprising that he found some saving resources in this desperate position. Pinter began with

74 g3

The idea is that after 74...hxg3+ 75 ♔xg3 White can play 76 ♘f4 and then advance the h-pawn. The black king can be driven off by ♖e1+ followed by ♖a1 when the rook helps force through the h-pawn. Kasparov found an excellent defence:

74 ... ♔e2!
75 ♖a1 f4!!

Attacking the g6 knight. This is by far Black's best chance though White retains an excellent position. We can run through a checklist which illustrates positional draws of more or less certainty:

i) White captures the h-pawn with his knight: 76 ♘xh4. Now 76...♗xh4? 77 gxh4 f3 78 ♖a2+ and 79 ♔g3 wins so Black must play 76...f3!.

(analysis diagram)

However, White can play a positional sacrifice 77 ♖a2+ ♔f1 (keeping the white king away from g1) 78 ♘xf3! ♗xf3 79 h4 and White can begin to advance his pawns. Black would have to play like a world champion to defend such a position.

ii) White captures the f-pawn: 76 ♘xf4+. Now 76...♔f2! 77 ♘h5 ♗e7 (77...hxg3+ 78 ♘xg3 ♗f4 79 ♖f1+ and 80 ♖e1+ wins).

(analysis diagram)

A bizarre position where it is difficult to see how White can escape from the bind of Black's pieces. For example, 78 ♖a7 ♗d6 79 ♖f7+ ♗f3 achieves nothing.

iii) White plays 76 gxh4! ♗h6 77 h5. White's best chance to win. The knight is defended and if he can neutralise the f-pawn then the h5 pawn will win the game.

iv) The game continuation.

76	♖a2+	♔e3
77	♖a3+	♔f2
78	gxf4	♗h6
79	♖a2+	♔f1
80	♖a1+	♔f2
81	♖g1	♔xg6
82	♖xg6	♗xf4+
83	♔h1	♗g3!

This was one of the positional draws for which Kasparov was angling. White cannot win, since he can never drive the black king out of the 'square' of the h-pawn. Therefore, a ♖xg3 or ♖xh4 sacrifice will never win.

The game continued: 84 ♔g4 ♖f1 85 ♔g5 ♔f2 86 ♖f5+ ♔e3 87 ♔g2 ♔e4 88 ♖f7 ♔d5 89 ♖e7 ♔d6 90 ♖e2 ♔d5 91 ♔f3 ♔d6 92 ♔g4 ♔d7 93 ♔f5 ♔d6 94 ♖e8 ♔d7 95 ♖e6 ♔c7 96 ♔e4 ♔d7 97 ♔d5 ♔c7 98 ♖e7+ ♔b6 99 ♖f7 ♗h2! (not 99...♔b5 100 ♖b7+ ♔a6 101 ♖b1 ♔a7 102 ♔e4 and White puts his king on g5 then plays ♖b4 and ♖xh4! winning the rook pawn when Black's king is too far away to stop the h-pawn

queening) 100 ♖f2 ♗g3 101 ♖c2 ♔b7 and White tried for another 16 moves to win before giving it up as a draw.

Thanks to knowledge of some endgame theory, the author managed to escape with a draw from the following unpleasant position:

McDonald-Shovel
London League 1994

Black played 47...♖h2 and was surprised when White answered 48 ♖f8 ♖xa2 49 ♖xf7 ♖a3. White has lost the b3 pawn, but the endgame after 50 ♔d4 ♖xb3 51 ♖f6+ ♔d7 52 ♔c4 is a theoretical draw.

The reader should aim to build up a large 'internal stock' of such standard draws. Often they will save him a great deal of analytical work, and sometimes they will save him the game.

3　Sacrifices to Create a Passed Pawn

Around the year 1500, the rules of chess underwent a dramatic change. The minister, the most pitiful piece on the board - a kind of circumscribed bishop only able to limp one square diagonally at a time - became *la dame enragée*, the modern aggressive omnipotent queen.

Suddenly, the tempo of chess speeded up: it was possible to be mated in two moves, when normally the two opposing armies did not come into contact for ten moves or so. All the established theory with its emphasis on patient, long drawn out positional manoeuvring, had to be discarded in the face of lightning attacks by the queen.

And yet, paradoxically, the strategy of chess had in other ways been enriched by this change of the queen's power. Previously, pawns could only be promoted into the feeble minister, a piece which had hardly any influence on the game. This meant that a pawn advantage or more in an endgame wasn't of much significance - and then suddenly there were 16 potential queens on the board! An extra pawn, or the *potential* to win a pawn in the endgame, assumed decisive importance.

Hence, positional play was deepened, since the slightest of advantages could eventually yield a win. The adage 'a pawn up in the endgame is quite enough to win' really means 'to checkmate you need at least a rook, and this comes about through being a pawn up, exchanging off the other pieces and pawns, and then queening the extra pawn'.

The worth of other pieces was also changed through empowering the queen and pawns. For example, to lose a knight for three pawns would often be a serious loss in the old game. Now, on the other hand, although a knight is nominally worth three pawns, in many situations, especially in the endgame, three healthy pawns can outweigh a knight. The capacity of the pawns to promote is the vital factor. Three pawns have the 'stored' energy of three queens; a knight is always a knight.

And similarly a pawn on the seventh rank is but a pawn; a pawn on the eighth rank is a queen! That is why games in which one player has sacrificed a piece or even a rook for several passed pawns often lead to mind-bending complications. If the defender succeeds in staving off the pawn advance, he wins; if not, he loses.

In this chapter, we begin with a technical (or 'no risk') sacrifice of the exchange to create passed pawns. Then, gradually more and more complex examples are introduced, where risk and imagination are as essential as calculation and knowledge.

Alekhine-Flohr
Nottingham 1936

In this position Alekhine sacrificed the exchange with 46 ♖xe6! and comments in the tournament book: 'One of the combinations that an experienced player does not need to calculate

to a finish. He *knows* that under given circumstances, the kingside pawns must become overwhelming.'

In other words, the sacrifice is not a risky venture, but a well-known technical device to drive home White's advantage. White would not make the sacrifice if there were any doubt about its value: after all, in the initial position he is a pawn up, with many different winning plans to choose from. 46 ♖xe6! is the quickest and cleanest way of finishing off the opponent. The rest of the game is self-explanatory: the pawns sweep all before them.

46	...	♗xe6
47	♗xe6	♖fb7
48	♗b3	♖e8

If 48...♖b5, White simply ignores the attack on the c-pawn and continues as in the game.

| 49 | h6 | gxh6 |
| 50 | g6! | |

An important moment. The white pawns are very strong in united formation, since they can protect each other as they edge forwards. 50 gxh6?? on the other hand would be a terrible positional mistake, since the pawns would become isolated and weak. In fact, in this case, Black could continue 50...♖h7 and immediately win one of the pawns. When advancing passed pawns, you should always try to keep them in a compact formation.

| 50 | ... | ♖g7 |
| 51 | f5 | ♖f8 |

52	♗c2!

Not 52 ♗f7? which gives Black the chance to counter-sacrifice with 52...♖xf7! when he has equal chances. The bishop and pawns are worth much more than a rook.

52	...	h5
53	♖d6	♖e7
54	f6	♖e1+
55	♔d2	♖f1
56	f7	h4
57	♖d7	1-0

58 g7 is threatened and if 57...♖g1 58 ♖e7 followed by 59 ♖e8+ wins.

Here is a more difficult modern example:

Davies-Onischuk
Budapest 1993

Black played:

26	...	♖exf5!
27	gxf5	♗xb2

Black now has two menacing connected passed pawns, while White's own passed pawns are doubled and ineffectual. Nigel Davies, the player of White in this game, is fully aware that if he does nothing active, it will be the same story as in the Alekhine game above: 'Under given circumstances, the passed pawns must become overwhelming, etc.' So instead of trying to directly stem the tide of the passed pawns, he launches a counterattack:

28	♖ae1	♘c5

28...♖xf5! looks a better way to kill off White's counterplay, e.g. 29 ♖e4 c3 30 ♖c4 (30 ♖g1 c2) 30...♘c5 31 ♖xb4 ♘d3 32 ♖b7+ ♔c8 or 32 ♖c4 ♖xf4+ 33 ♖xf4 ♘xf4 34 ♔xf4 c2 and wins.

29	♖e6!

White sacrifices the exchange himself in order to turn his passed pawns into a potent force. Unfortunately, it does not prove enough to save the game, but it is still the best fighting chance.

29	...	♘xe6?

Better is 29...♖xf5!? 30 ♖xd6+ ♔e7, when both 31 ♖c6 ♘d3 32 ♖xc4 ♘e5+ 33 ♔e4 ♖xf4+! 34 ♔xf4 ♘xc4 and 31 ♖e1+ ♔f7 32 ♖c6 ♖xf4+ 33 ♔xf4 ♘d3+ win.

30	fxe6+	♔e7
31	♔e4	b3

Continuing as in Alekhine-Flohr with 31...♖xf4+ is not clear, e.g. 32 ♔xf4 c3 33 ♔e3 c2 34 ♔d2 b3 35 f4!? ♗d4 36 ♔c1 and the pawns are stymied.

32	♗e3	a6
33	♗d4	♗xd4
34	♔xd4	b2

Now an interesting rook and pawn endgame results. Black has

to play with great accuracy to win.

35 &b1

If 35 &xc4 &xf2 and the double threat of 36...&xh2 and 36...&c2+ followed by 37...&c1 forces White to transpose into the game continuation.

35	...	&xf2
36	&xc4	&xh2
37	&f1	h5

White has no answer to this passed pawn.

38	&f7+	&e8
39	&b7	h4
40	&b8+	&e7
41	&d3	h3
42	&b7+	&f6
43	&f7+	&g6
44	&f1	&g2!
45	e7	b1(&)+
46	&xb1	&f7

Material is now equal, but the e7 pawn is easily neutralised by the black king. Meanwhile, the black h-pawn is very strong, and if White tries to approach it with his king, he will lose both his a-pawn and his d-pawn.

47 &e3

If 47 &e1 &e8 and Black's rook starts by gobbling the a-pawn.

47	...	&a2
48	&f4	&xe7
49	&b7+	&f6
50	&b6	&f2+!

Freeing the g5 square for the king.

51	&g3	h2
52	&xd6+	&g5
53	&xf2	h1(&)

54	&xa6	&h2+
55	&f1	&h3+
	0-1	

The rook is lost after 56 &g1 &g3+ 57 &h1 &e1+ 58 &h2 &e2+ or 56 &e1 &e3+ followed by ...&d3+.

In the above games, the exchange was sacrificed with the simple and direct aim of forcing through the pawns to the queening square. In the following example, the *threat* of queening is used as a diversionary tactic to pin down the defender's pieces and make him unable to resist an attack on the other wing.

I.Sokolov-Riemersma
Leeuwarden 1993

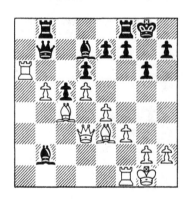

Here White played:

| 21 | &c6 | &xc6 |
| 22 | dxc6 | &c7 |

White now has two strong and completely unassailable passed pawns. Black will never be able to arrange a ...&xb5 counter-sacrifice or dislodge the white bishop with ...d6-d5 (assuming of course that White remains vigilant). Therefore, White's sacrifice is excellent in that he can hardly lose.

But how is White to win? The queenside is blocked and Black's bishop controls the a1 square, so White cannot hope to penetrate along the a-file. The passed pawns, although strong, can be firmly blocked on the dark squares in front of them. However, two factors are in White's favour:

i) The black queen, although doing an excellent job blocking the passed pawns, is shut away from the centre and the kingside. The rook on b8 also cannot venture too far from the b-file.

ii) The recapture 22 dxc6 has opened up the a2-g8 diagonal for White's bishop. The f7 square could become vulnerable.

So White decided he should begin an attack on the kingside. The potential threat from the queenside pawns ties down a large part of Black's army and impedes his mobility.

| 23 | f4 | ♖a8 |

Black is afraid of White's attack and so forces an exchange of rooks. The problem of course is that Black now has fewer pieces to block the pawns and defend his kingside.

24	♖b1	♖a1
25	♖xa1	♗xa1
26	f5	

The first direct threat: 27 fxg6 hxg6 28 e5 ♗xe5? 29 ♕xg6+.

| 26 | ... | ♗e5 |
| 27 | g3 | ♖e8 |

Black flounders about, unable to find a good plan. 27...♕a7 was better, though Black remains passive.

| 28 | ♕b3 | |

Now White plans 29 ♕a2 followed by ♗a5 to force through his queenside pawns.

| 28 | ... | ♖f8 |
| 29 | ♔g2! | |

There is no reason to hurry. Black can do nothing, so why not wait and see if he self-destructs?

| 29 | ... | ♕b6 |
| 30 | ♗h6! | |

Forcing the black bishop to a worse square before embarking on his queenside action.

| 30 | ... | ♗g7 |
| 31 | ♗d2 | |

Now White is ready to carry out his plan of 32 ♕a2 and 33 ♗a5.

| 31 | ... | gxf5 |
| 32 | exf5 | ♗e5 |

To answer 33 ♕a2 with 33...d5! when Black breaks free. But now disaster strikes on the other side.

33	♗h6	♗g7
34	♗xg7!	♔xg7
35	♕e3	e6

Sokolov gives the variation 35...♕c7 36 ♕g5+ ♔h8 37 ♕h6 ♔g8 38 f6! exf6 39 ♗d3 ♖e8 40 ♗xh7+ ♔h8 41 b6!! which demonstrates the two facets of White's winning scheme: kingside attack and queenside pawn advances.

36	♕g5+	♔h8
37	♕f6+	♔g8
38	fxe6	1-0

Black's game collapses.

We shall now look at some examples in which a piece is sacrificed to create passed pawns. A piece is of course a much greater material investment than the exchange, and so the compensation must be proportionally more tangible and 'tactical'. The following game is given in its entirety since it demonstrates how a sacrifice can flow logically out of the strategical requirements of a position.

Yusupov-Christiansen
Las Palmas 1993

1	d4	d6
2	e4	♘f6
3	f3	e5
4	dxe5	dxe5
5	♕xd8+	♔xd8
6	♗c4	♗e6
7	♗xe6	fxe6

Black has blunted any aggressive intentions White may have had. He hopes that the e-pawns, although doubled and isolated, will prove defensible since they cannot be frontally attacked. Yusupov, however, finds a way to begin a siege of the e5 pawn:

8   ♘h3!

With the idea of ♘f2-d3, per-

haps combining with ♘d2-c4 and ♗d2-c3, putting intense pressure on e5.

8	...	♗c5
9	♘f2	♗xf2+
10	♔xf2	

So Black has prevented ♘d3, but at the cost of exchanging his long-range bishop for the knight. White's bishop on c1 now looks like the best minor piece on the board.

| 10 | ... | ♘c6 |
| 11 | ♗e3 | ♔e7 |

12   ♘a3!

Another sideways deployment of a knight (see move 8), and another exclamation mark. The idea is to play c3, depriving the black knight on c6 of the central d4 square, and then re-route the knight from a3 to c5 via c2, e1 and d3. Such a slow manoeuvre is perfectly feasible in view of the fixed and static nature of the position.

12   ...   a6?!

Black wants to centralise his rooks without being bothered by the possibility of ♘b5. However, this careless pawn move was exactly what White was hoping for. 12...♖ad8 was better, when if 13 ♘b5 a6 14 ♘xc7? ♖d7 15 ♗b6 ♖c8 wins the knight. After 12...♖ad8 13 c3 ♖d7 followed by ...♖hd8 Black would have had a safe position.

| 13 | c3 | ♖hd8 |
| 14 | ♔e2 | h6 |

Another superfluous pawn move. 14...♖d7 was better.

| 15 | ♘c2 | ♖d7 |
| 16 | ♖hd1 | ♖ad8 |

Imagine if Black had not wasted a move on 12...a6, but had instead played to double his rooks on the d-file immediately. In that case, we would reach virtually the game position with Black to move. Black could then exchange off both pairs of rooks with excellent drawing chances. White in fact wants to exchange *one* rook to rule out any Black activity down the d-file. He does not want to exchange off *both* rooks since he needs a rook to support his strategy. (This will become apparent in what follows.) Therefore, if Yusupov had wished to play for advantage against correct play by Black, he would have been forced to leave the black rooks unchallenged on the d-file. A little lost time can be fatal in chess, even in 'quiet' positions.

17	♖xd7+	♖xd7
18	♘e1!	♘e8
19	♘d3	♘d6

Managing to bolster the b-pawn before ♘c5. So White switches his thoughts back to the e-pawn.

| 20 | ♗f2! | b6 |

White's plan is to play ♗g3 and then b4, a4, ♖b1 and b5, forcing away the c6 knight and winning the e5 pawn. Here we see why White retained one rook - a rook is necessary to support the undermining queenside pawn advance. So Black tries to set up a pawn barricade but it further weakens his queenside pawns.

| 21 | ♗g3 | ♘f7 |
| 22 | a4 | a5 |

So that if 23 b4? axb4 24 cxb4 ♘d4+ and the knight is well centralised.

| 23 | ♖c1! | ♔f6 |
| 24 | b4 | |

White offers to concede the d4 square to Black's knight since after 24...axb4 25 cxb4 ♘d4+ 26 ♔e3 he has a strong potential passed pawn on the a-file, and the e5 pawn is still vulnerable. Yusupov gives the following variation in *Informator 58*: 26...c6 27 a5 bxa5 28 bxa5 ♖a7 29 ♘xe5! ♘xe5 30 ♗xe5+ ♔xe5 31 ♖c5+ with a winning position.

| 24 | ... | ♖d8 |

Black decides to wait patiently. However, White can now prepare a breakthrough on the c-file.

| 25 | b5 | ♘e7 |
| 26 | ♗f2! | |

A little care is needed. 26 c4 c5! 27 bxc6 ♘xc6 (Yusupov) would leave the black knight eyeing d4. But now of course,

26...c5? would lose the b-pawn.

26   ...   ♖b8

So Black defends the b-pawn.

27   c4   c5

The only way to stop White breaking through with c5, cxb6 and ♗c7.

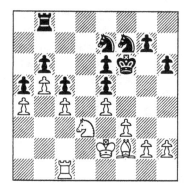

If now 28 bxc6 then 28...♘xc6 29 ♖b1 ♘d6! (attacking c4) is satisfactory for Black. And if the position remains blocked, then Black can claim that his knight is better than White's impeded bishop. Instead White played:

28   ♘xc5

It would be strange if White's well thought out and well executed plan suddenly led to a strategical 'dead-end' and he had to think about equalising the game. Chess is normally (though not always) a logical game. Therefore, a sacrifice on c5, giving up a piece for two pawns, is neither speculation nor a 'lucky find'. There is nothing fortuitous about discovering a winning sacrifice in a position which has been carefully nurtured according

to the laws of strategy. And furthermore, the sacrifice is not a luxury which can be played or declined according to the player's style or state of mind (i.e. whether he is feeling brave or not). It *must* be played. In fact, as Yusupov points out, 28 ♗xc5! was even stronger. After 28...bxc5 29 ♘xc5 ♖a8 30 ♘d7+ followed by 31 c5, etc., the pawns sweep through. The reason why 28 ♘xc5 is inferior will soon become clear.

28   ...   bxc5
29   ♗xc5   ♘d8
30   ♗d6   ♖b7
31   ♖d1

The first sign that it is not easy for White. The 'obvious' 31 c5 allows 31...♘ec6! 32 bxc6 (in fact, 32 ♔d3 is better, in reply to which the knight stands its ground on c6) 32...♖b2+ 33 ♔f1 ♘xc6. White is a pawn up, but the black knight is excellently placed on c6, blocking the passed pawn. And we see the limitations of a bishop well illustrated: it only controls squares of one colour, and the view from d6 is not very good - it is virtually incarcerated by its own pawn on c5 and Black's e5 pawn and knight. Imagine if the bishop on d6 were a knight. It could easily escape from its prison, jumping over other pieces if necessary (whether friend or foe). The c6 square would not be a 'no-go area' either, since the knight could conspire with the rook to oust its opposite number.

| 31 | ... | ♘dc6 |

Black still makes the sacrifice, but in far less favourable circumstances - the white bishop is not blocked in by his c5 pawn, and the white rook is more actively placed. However, the sacrifice was probably necessary sooner or later.

| 32 | bxc6 | ♘xc6 |
| 33 | ♗c5 | |

Keeping the knight out of d4 and preparing to penetrate with his rook.

33	...	♖b2+
34	♖d2	♖b3
35	♖d6	♘e7?

According to Yusupov, the last chance for Black was 35...♘d4+! 36 ♗xd4 exd4 37 ♖xd4 ♖b4. Black wins the a-pawn and is left 'only' a pawn down in a rook and pawn endgame. This would have been the way for Black to punish White for his wrong choice of sacrifice at move 28.

| 36 | ♗b6 | ♘g6 |

36...♘c8 fails to 37 ♗d8+ and 38 ♖c6. Black soon loses his a-pawn and his 'counter-attack' proves fruitless against the passed a- and c-pawns.

| 37 | ♗xa5 | ♘f4+ |
| 38 | ♔d2 | ♘xg2 |

38...♖a3 39 ♗d8+ and 40 a5 wins.

39	c5	♘e3
40	♗d8+	♔f7
41	♖d3	

Avoiding all tricks. Black could already resign.

41	...	♘c4+
42	♔c2	♖b8
43	c6	♔e8
45	♖c3	♘b6
46	a5	♖xa5

46...♘c8 47 ♖c5 is hopeless.

| 47 | c8(♕) | 1-0 |

The strategical course of the game above was fairly clear. In the following example, difficult tactical variations obscure the logical flow of the game as White battles to prove the correctness of his sacrifice.

Serper-Nikolaidis
St Petersburg 1993

Black should play 15...♘f4 followed by 16...0-0 with a reasonable game. Instead he tried:

| 15 | ... | ♘f8 |

with the laudable intention of manoeuvring his knight to the excellent d4 square. He had mistakenly assumed that because the position is semi-closed, White cannot exploit the time he wastes in retreating the knight. Serper, on the other hand, is alert to his chances of striking a quick blow before Black is able to castle. He begins with:

16   a4!   b4

This provokes the sacrifice, but 16...bxa4 17 ♖xa4 intending 18 ♖fa1 would be positional suicide.

17   ♘d5!   cxd5

Again forced, since otherwise he loses the b-pawn. It is better to face a huge attack than be a pawn down for nothing - any sacrifice carries an element of risk for the sacrificer.

18   exd5

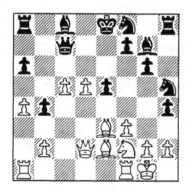

White's compensation for the piece is obvious. Even if Black's pieces were on good squares and his king safe, it would be difficult to prevent the united passed pawns from rampaging down the board. But as it is, with Black's rook sitting uselessly on the wings, his minor pieces disorganised, and his king stuck in the centre, only one verdict is possible: White has a winning advantage.

18   ...   f5!

A valiant attempt to keep the white knight out of e4 (the threat was ♘e4-d6+). The black rook on h8 may one day be able to swing to the centre of the board via h7. Also, 19...f4, winning the bishop on e3, is introduced as a threat. The obvious defensive idea would be to move the knight on f8 and castle. However, all knight moves fail:

i) 18...♘d7 19 ♘e4 0-0 20 ♖ac1 and White is ready to push Black off the board with c5-c6 and d5-d6.

ii) 18...♘e6 19 dxe6 ♗xe6 20 ♕xb4 0-0. Black's king is safe but he is a pawn down.

iii) 18...♘f4 19 ♘e4 (better than 19 ♗xf4 exf4 20 ♘e4 ♗e5! intending ...♘h7 and ...0-0) 19...♘xe2+ 20 ♕xe2 followed by ♘d6+ with a strong attack.

19   d6   ♕c6

Serper points out in *Die Schachwoche* that 19...♕d7 20 c6! ♕xc6 21 ♖fc1 ♕d7 22 ♖c7 wins. The black queen is curiously short of squares and will be lost to ♖e7+.

(see following diagram)

Now it seems as if the pawns are blockaded, but Serper has another surprise waiting:

20   ♗b5!!

Once again a sacrifice to convert a closed position into an open one. Black is never allowed the one tempo he needs to play ...♘e6 or ...♘d7 and ...0-0.

20   ...   axb5

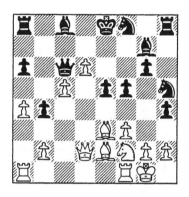

21 axb5 ♕xb5

Or 21...♕b7 22 c6 ♕b8 23 b6 (a very aesthetic array of pawns) 23...♘f6 24 ♕xb4 ♘d5 25 ♕b5 ♘xe3 (25...♖xa1 26 c7+!) 26 ♖xa8 ♕xa8 27 b7 ♕b8 28 c7+. A variation which demonstrates the enormous power of the passed pawns.

22 ♖xa8 ♕c6
23 ♖fa1

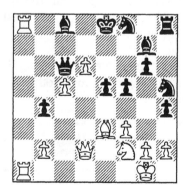

23 ... f4

Black decides he may as well be hanged for a sheep as for a lamb. The attempt to develop with 23...♘d7 fails to 24 ♖xc8+!

♕xc8 25 ♕d5 stopping castling and threatening ♖a8 or c5-c6; for example 25...♘hf6 (25...♘df6 26 ♕xe5+) 26 ♕e6+ ♔f8 27 ♘d3 (threatening ♘xe5) 27...e4 28 ♘f4 ♕e8 29 ♖a8! ♕xa8 30 ♘xg6 mate. A better defensive try is 23...♗f6 intending to answer 24 ♖a1-a7 with ...♖h7! activating his rook. However, 24 ♕xb4 ♖h7 25 ♖a1-a6! looks decisive.

24 ♖1a7 ♘d7
24...fxe3 25 ♕d5!! is devastating.

25 ♖xc8+!
Under no circumstances must Black be allowed to castle.

25 ... ♕xc8
26 ♕d5 fxe3
27 ♕e6+
Not 27 ♘e4 ♘f4!.

27 ... ♔f8
28 ♖xd7 exf2+
29 ♔f1
Bad is 29 ♔xf2? ♕xc5+.

Despite Black's two extra pieces, he has no good defence. Serper gives the variation 29...♘g3+ 30 hxg3 ♕xd7 31

♕xd7 hxg3 (threatening ...♖h1+, queening) 32 ♕e7+ ♚g8 33 ♕e8+ ♗f8 34 ♕xg6+ followed by ♕xg3, and White wins. We can add another interesting variation: 29...♕a6+ 30 ♚xf2 ♕e2+!? 31 ♚xe2 ♘f4+ 32 ♚d1 ♘xe6 33 c6 and White wins after 33...♚e8 34 ♖a7 ♗f6 35 ♖a8+ followed by 36 ♖xh8 and 37 c7, or 36 c7 immediately, as appropriate. Or if 33...♚g8 34 ♖e7 ♚h7 35 ♖xe6 and wins - the passed pawns march through. The last variation demonstrates the enormous power of the passed pawns.

| 29 | ... | ♕e8 |
| 30 | ♖f7+! | |

Yet another sacrifice to clear the way for the pawns.

30	...	♕xf7
31	♕c8+	♕e8
32	d7!	

Black now has the huge material advantage of a rook, bishop and knight for a pawn - but what a pawn! Black must now give up his queen.

32	...	♚f7
33	dxe8(♕)+	♖xe8
34	♕b7+	♖e7
35	c6!	e4

Although Black still has a nominal material advantage, his pieces are too disorganised to stop the c-pawn.

| 36 | c7 | e3 |

A last desperate fling by Black. Perhaps White will play 37 c8(♕) and allow 37...e2+ 38 ♚xf2 e1(♕) mate?

37	♕d5+	♚f6
38	♕d6+	♚f7
39	♕d5+	♚f6
40	♕d6+	♚f7

A little repetition in time pressure. Now White plays the winning move.

| 41 | ♕xe7+ | ♚xe7 |
| 42 | c8(♕) | |

The c- and d-pawns have had a glorious career. One cost Black his queen, the other became (and stayed) a queen.

42	...	♗h6
43	♕c5+	♚e8
44	♕b5+	♚d8
45	♕b6+	♚d7
46	♕xg6	e2+

Hoping White will capture the wrong pawn and lose his queen to a knight fork.

| 47 | ♚xf2! | ♗e3+ |
| 48 | ♚e1 | 1-0 |

The board was not showered with gold coins after this fantastic display, but Serper did receive 250,000 roubles for the Best Game prize.

Our final example is a complicated struggle in which both sides acquire passed pawns.

Teske-P.Szilagyi
Budapest 1991

(see diagram overleaf)

White can claim a very small advantage in this arid-looking position: his rook controls the only open file. However, Black has only to play ...♗b7 and ...♖c8, exchanging rooks, and any advantage will completely vanish. Evidently Teske did not like the look of 22 罩xc8+ 罩xc8 23 豐xa6 罩c2, when 24 奧c1 (24 ②d3? 罩xe2) 24...罩xa2 or 24...豐c7!? is unclear, so he played:

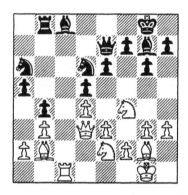

22 罩c6

expecting Black to move to defend his knight. Instead, Black played the highly ingenious

22 ... 豐d7!!

letting White carry out his threat. Actually White should now retreat his rook, with an equal position. However, this would be a psychologically difficult decision to make, so White accepts the challenge.

23 罩xa6? ②c4!

Now after 24 bxc4 奧xa6 followed by 25...dxc4 Black's passed pawns would steam-roller through the queenside. For example, 24 bxc4 奧xa6 25 豐b1 dxc4 26 奧e4 豐b5 27 d5 c3 28 奧c1 exd5 29 奧xd5 a4 followed by ...b4-b3 and wins. So White prepares a counter-sacrifice to

obtain some passed pawns of his own.

24	罩a7	豐xa7
25	bxc4	奧a6
26	②xd5!	

This should not save the game but it is the best try.

26	...	exd5
27	奧xd5	

Now things do not seem so bad for White. He has connected passed pawns in the centre and an active bishop. As yet, Black has no passed pawns of his own, and the rook on b8 has no open file. However, if we look more closely at the position, we will see that White's pieces are in fact on vulnerable squares. This is almost entirely due to the pressure of Black's bishop on a6 which terrorises the c4 pawn. If White could evacuate his queen from d3 and achieve the advance c5 without losing his knight on e2 or his bishop on d5, or indeed the pawn on c4 itself, then he would have a safe game. But this is not easy to achieve, especially if Black plays

27...罝c8!. This threatens 28...豐c7 winning the c-pawn. The only reply is 28 豐c2 but then 28...奧xc4 29 奧xc4 豐c7 30 奧xf7+ 含xf7 31 豐e4 (31 豐b3+ 豐c4) 31...含g8 with the idea of ...豐c2 looks very strong.

Alternatively, Black could play 27...豐d7 threatening 28...豐xd5. Now 28 豐b3 a4! or 28 豐e4 罝c8 or finally 28 ⃞f4 g5! are all bad for White. However, 28 e4! holds on, though Black is better, e.g. after 28...豐xh3!?.

Black played an inferior move in the game:

| 27 | ... | 豐c7?! |
| 28 | 豐c2 | |

Now 28...罝c8 can be answered by 29 c5 when White has achieved his central pawn advance.

| 28 | ... | 豐d7 |
| 29 | ⃞f4? | |

White does not take advantage of Black's hesitancy. He should retreat his bishop to g2 and then play c4-c5, perhaps followed by d4-d5 and c5-c6. This would activate his passed pawns.

29	...	a4
30	⃞d3	b3
31	axb3	axb3
32	豐c3	豐d6!

To answer 33 ⃞c5 with 33...豐xc5! winning. 32...豐xh3 33 ⃞c5 奧c8 34 ⃞xb3, on the other hand, would be unclear.

| 33 | ⃞e5 | |

The culmination of White's mistaken plan which began with 29 ⃞f4. It was still not too late to

play 33 奧g2 and 34 c5. White has wasted three moves preparing to bring the knight into an attacking position on the kingside when the correct strategy was the advance of his passed pawns.

| 33 | ... | 豐b4! |
| 34 | 奧xf7+ | |

34 豐f1 was the last chance.

| 34 | ... | 含f8 |
| 35 | 豐c1 | |

This is White's idea. Unfortunately he has underestimated the strength of Black's passed pawn.

| 35 | ... | 奧xe5 |
| 36 | 奧a3 | |

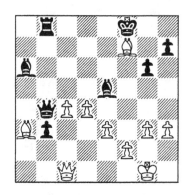

| 36 | ... | 奧d6? |

Here 36...含xf7 wins (but not 36...b2? 37 豐xb2!), e.g. 37 奧xb4 罝xb4 38 豐b2 (38 dxe5 b2 39 豐b1 奧xc4 40 含h2 罝b7! followed by ...奧d3 wins, or 38 豐a3 罝b8! 39 豐xa6 b2 wins) 38...奧c7 39 c5 (39 豐a3 罝b6 40 c5 b2) 39...奧b7 followed by ...奧d5 and ...罝a5-a2, etc. forcing the pawns through. Evidently Black became confused in time pressure.

| 37 | 奧xb4 | 罝xb4 |

38	♗d5	b2
39	♕b1	♗c7

Black plans to put his bishop on c3 and then play ...♖a4 and ...♖a1 ousting the white queen. White's passed pawns do not seem dangerous at present: if White ever plays c4-c5, then ...♗d3! will be the instant riposte. So is Black still winning after all? Unfortunately for Black, another factor has become important: king safety. The white bishop on d5 and the queen would be a deadly force against Black's exposed king; assuming of course the queen can free itself of blockading duties...

40	♔g2!	♗a5

Carrying on with his plan. An attempt to flee with the king fails, e.g. 40...♔g7 41 ♕e4! b1(♕) 42 ♕e7+ ♔h6 43 ♕f8+ ♔h5 44 ♗f3+ ♔g5 45 h4 mate.

41	c5!	♗d3

Black had no choice, since 41 c5 opened not only the a6-f1 diagonal but also the a2-g8 diagonal: 42 ♗a2! followed by ♕e4 was threatened.

42	♕xd3	b1(♕)
43	♕a6!	

Despite his extra rook, Black is lost. 43...♗d8 can be answered by 44 ♕e6! when 44...♖b7 45 ♕g8+ ♔e7 46 ♕f7 is mate, or 44...♕f5 45 ♕g8+ ♔e7 46 ♕g7+ ♔e8 47 ♗c6 mates, or if 44...♔g7 45 ♕f7+ leads to a mate similar to that given at move 40. Since White is threatening 44 ♕f6+ ♔e8 45 ♗c6 mate, Black has no choice but to return a piece, but this is hopeless as well. No doubt he was feeling somewhat aggrieved, and with good reason.

43	...	♕f5
44	e4	♕g5
45	♕xa5	♖b2
46	♕a8+	♔e7
47	♕a7+	♔d8
48	♕f7	1-0

Even if he avoids being mated, a rook is no match for a bishop and four passed pawns.

An exciting and instructive game, despite its flaws. It illustrates very well that when there are passed pawns, the value of pieces can fluctuate enormously.

4 Sacrifices to Destroy the Opponent's Centre

One day, scientists may discover a manageable formula to find the 'best' move in any chess position. If they do, then part of the equation will undoubtedly address the question of central control. Many opening and middlegame moves appear meaningless or bizarre until one realises that their aim is to seize control of the centre or prevent the opponent from doing so. Control of the centre gives the pieces extra mobility and opens up all sorts of possibilities of attack.

It is no wonder, therefore, that the sacrifice to destroy or weaken the opponents centre is one of the most common themes in positional chess. In fact, such sacrifices are so frequent that they should be in every player's armoury.

In a single chapter it is not possible to classify and illustrate every example of this sacrificial motif, so we shall restrict ourselves to looking at some specific instances. First, we will examine some cases where White or Black sacrifices the exchange on his opponents K3 (e6 or e3) for positional compensation.

Hulak-Gabriel
Slovenia 1993

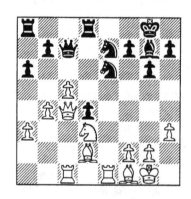

At first glance, Black appears to have a safe and solid position. However, White completely disrupted Black's position with the sacrifice 28 ♖xe6! fxe6 29 ♘f4!. There is no answer to the threat of 30 ♘xe6. Black tried 29...b5 but lost quickly after 30 cxb6 ♕xc4 31 ♗xc4 ♗h6 32 b7 ♖ab8 33 ♘xe6 ♗xd2 24 ♘xd8+ ♔h8

35 ♘f7+ ♔g7 36 ♖d1 ♗c3 37 ♘d6 ♘f5 38 ♘xf5+ gxf5 39 ♗xa6 and Black resigned.

A fairly simple example: Black was defenceless after the sacrifice since he had no answer to the tactical threats. We now consider a more heavyweight positional battle, where chances are more evenly balanced.

Raecky-Krasenkov
Rostov on Don 1993

White played:
20 ♖xe6   fxe6
Assuming that the e6 pawn is doomed, White has sacrificed a rook for a bishop and pawn. His compensation:

i) Black's pawn centre is shattered, and his kingside weakened. Black could have serious problems on the a2-g8 diagonal from an attack by White's queen and knight. (This actually occurs in the game.)

ii) White has eliminated Black's pair of bishops which were becoming menacing. As is well known, two bishops are often stronger than a bishop and knight, especially when they are on aligned diagonals and the centre is open (which was the case before White's sacrifice here).

iii) The disappearance of Black's bishop pair and the disruption of his centre has taken a lot of the dynamism out of Black's position. It is hard to imagine Black carrying out a successful kingside attack, for instance. Therefore, White's static or long-term advantage is now of much more value, since Black has little active counterplay.

However, we should not overestimate White's position. He certainly has compensation for the exchange, but we cannot yet speak of a clear advantage, let alone a win. White merely has a safe game and the initiative. The player who shows the best qualities in the resulting struggle will win.

21 h4
White is in no hurry to capture the e-pawn. First, he makes an escape square for his king, should he ever be checked on the back rank (which happens a couple of moves later), and introduces the idea of h4-h5, further weakening Black's kingside.

21 ...   ♔h8
22 ♘e4   ♖f8
Black must play cautiously. If 22...♖bd8 23 ♕xe6 ♕xa4 24

 Øg5 threatens a smothered mate after 25 Øf7+ ⚔g8 26 Øh6+ ⚔h8 27 ♕g8+! and 28 Øf7 mate.

23 ♖d1

This leads to a favourable exchange of rooks for Black, whose queen is then poised to enter into active play with a check on White's back rank. In his notes in *Informator 58*, Raecky says he was afraid to play 23 ♗h3 because of 23...♗d4 with the threat of 24...♗xf2+ 25 Øxf2 ♖xf2+ 26 ⚔xf2 ♕d2+ winning the rook on c1. However, 23...♗d4 could be met by 24 ⚔g2! when 24...♗xf2? fails to 25 ♕b2+ followed by 26 Øxf2 winning. Black could answer 24 ⚔g2 with 24...e5 but then after 25 ♖d1 White keeps a slight advantage. He can prepare to queen a pawn on the queenside (c5-c6) or attack on the kingside (h4-h5). The difference between this variation and the game continuation is that Black's queen remains shut out of the game on a5.

23 ... ♖bd8

24 ♖xd8 ♕xd8
25 ♕xe6 ♕d1+

Black has achieved a great deal. His queen is reactivated and he has exchanged a pair of rooks. As a general rule, if the opponent has sacrificed or lost the exchange, the defender should aim to exchange off the other rook.

26 ⚔h2 ♕xa4
27 ♕xe7

This is good enough for equality. The attempt to play for advantage with 27 c6 rebounds after 27...bxc6 28 bxc6 ♕c2 29 ♕d7 a5 30 c7 a4 (not 30...♗e5 31 ♕xe7 winning) 31 ♗h3 a3 (but not 31...♕xe4 32 c8(♕) ♖xc8 33 ♕xc8 mates) and the black pawn runs through to queen.

27 ... ♕xb5
28 Ød6 ♕b3

Of course, taking the c-pawn loses the queen. 28...♕b2 29 f4 ♕f6 30 ♕xb7 is unclear, says Raecky.

29 f4 a5

Now Black also has a dangerous passed pawn. A race develops.

30 ♗xb7 a4
31 c6 a3
32 c7 ♕c2+!

Not 32...a2 33 c8(♕) ♖xc8 34 ♗xc8 threatening 35 ♕e8+ ♕g8 36 Øf7 mate.

33 ⚔h3 a2
34 c8(♕) ♕xc8+!

Well played. 34...♖xc8 35 ♗xc8 h5 (36 ♕e8+ was threatened) 36 ♗e6 leads to a quick mate, e.g. 36...a1(♕) 37 ♕e8+

♔h7 38 ♕g8+ ♔h6 39 ♘f7 mate.

35 ♗xc8 a1(♕)
36 ♘f7+?

After such an exciting struggle, White, no doubt in time pressure, carries on playing for a win when it was time to settle for equality. Here he should have played 36 ♗b7 when 36...♕a7 (pinning the bishop) 37 ♘f7+ ♔g8 38 ♘h6+! ♔h8 (not 38...♗xh6? 39 ♗d5+ winning the queen) 39 ♘f7+ is perpetual check.

36 ... ♔g8
37 ♗e6 ♕h1+

Driving the king out. Of course, if White had played 36 ♗b7 this would have been impossible.

38 ♔g4

38 ... h5+?

Here it is Black's turn to go wrong. We should remember that chess players, even Russian grandmasters, are not automatons but flesh and blood, prone to nervousness and error. Krasenkov points out that 38...♕g2! was

very strong. This threatens 39...h5+ followed by ...♕xg3+ and mate. After 39 ♘e5+ ♔h8 40 ♕a3 (there is nothing else) 40...h5+ 41 ♔g5 ♔h7 (threatening 42...♗h6 or 42...♗f6 mate) 42 ♘xg6 ♖f6, White has to play 43 f5 ♖xe6 44 fxe6 ♕d5+ when Black wins the knight, with excellent winning chances. Similar is 43 ♗f5 ♖xf5+ 44 ♔xf5 ♕c2+, again winning the knight. We may add another variation to Krasenkov's analysis: 43 ♕d3 ♕xg3+!! 44 ♕xg3 ♖xg6+ and wins. Interestingly, Raecky did not see the strength of 38...♕g2 even in his home analysis. According to his notes given in *Informator*, White was always at least equal throughout the course of the game.

39 ♔g5 ♔h7
40 g4 ♕g1

Raecky mentions 40...♕d1, a nasty move which threatens 41...♖xf7 42 ♕xf7 ♕d8 mating, or if 42 ♗xf7 ♕xg4 mate. White had to play 41 ♘e5 when 41...♕d8 (or 41...♕d6! forcing the same reply) 42 ♘xg6 ♕xe7 43 ♘xe7 ♗f6+ 44 ♔xh5 ♗xe7 45 f5 is an interesting material balance - rook and bishop against bishop and three passed pawns. After 45...♖a8 46 g5 White will sooner or later play f5-f6, when Black will have to play ...♗xf6 with a drawn endgame (otherwise the passed pawns would be too strong).

41 ♘e5

41   ...   ♛b1

When Krasenkov played 40...♛g1, he may have planned 41...♛c5 here. The queen is taboo because of 42...♝f6 or 42...♝h6 mate, and 42 ♛b7 ♛b6! 43 ♛d7 ♛xe6! 44 ♛xe6 ♝h6 mate does not help. But White has the devilish move 42 ♝g8+!! and after 42...♚xg8 or 42...♜xg8, White can safely capture Black's queen and there is no mate. If it were not for the 'flukey' 42 ♝g8+, all Black's previous moves would be justified, and Krasenkov would have scored a fine victory. We may talk about positional chess, but unexpected tactical strokes are always lurking there to upset the logical flow of the game. Incredibly, instead of 41...♛b1, Black should force a draw with 41...♜xf4! 42 ♚xf4 ♛d4+ followed by capturing the knight.

42   ♘d7!   ♜a8?

Evidently the struggle has proved too much for Black. As Raecky points out, he could still draw with 42...♜xf4! 43 ♚xf4

♛f1+ 44 ♚e4 ♛g2+ 45 ♚d3 ♛f1+ 46 ♚c2 ♛e2+ 47 ♚b3 ♛b5+ and White's king cannot escape perpetual check. Perhaps Black was still looking for the elusive win.

43   ♝d5!   hxg4

Black's last chance, threatening 44...♛f5 mate. Hopeless is 43...♛b5 44 f5! ♛b1 (44...♛xd5? 45 ♘f6+) 45 ♘f6+ ♚h8 46 ♚xg6, or 43...♜c8 44 ♘f6+ ♚h8 45 ♘e8.

44   ♘f6+   ♚h8
45   ♝e4!   1-0

The killer move. Now Raecky gives 45...♛a1 46 ♝xa8 ♛xa8 47 ♚xg6 ♛f8 48 ♛xf8 ♝xf8 49 ♘xg4 and wins. It is ironic that the white king, which Black had been hunting down, is transformed into a strong attacking piece. Despite the mistakes, this was an absorbing struggle.

In the game above, although the initial sacrifice was based mainly on an assessment of positional factors, there were some difficult tactical variations to calculate. In the following struggle, Tiviakov playing Black makes the mirror image of White's sacrifice on e6. This time, however, the battle is decided by verbal 'stream of consciousness' reasoning rather than a mass of variations.

Razuvaev-Tiviakov
Rostov on Don 1993

Evidently Rostov on Don is a

happy breeding ground for positional exchange sacrifices. Here Tiviakov played:

| 15 | ... | ♖xe3! |
| 16 | fxe3 | d6 |

What has Black gained for his sacrifice?

i) White's e-pawns are in the worst formation possible - doubled and for all intents isolated (since the d5 pawn won't ever help their defence). Furthermore, they stand on an open file. The e3 pawn has the choice of being weak on e3 or e4.

ii) The black knight gains the beautiful central square e5 where it is completely unassailable. (However, it should be pointed out that the black knight shields the white e-pawns from frontal attack, so Black will not automatically place it there.)

iii) Black has an absolutely solid pawn structure. Rooks thrive on open files, yet White only has one semi-open file, the f-file, and Black has time to fortify it. In what follows, White

may try c4-c5, giving up a pawn in order to open the b-file for his rooks (or the d-file if Black answers c4-c5 with ...dxc5 and White then plays d5-d6). So Black will be vigilant: he will make sure that c4-c5 is either prevented or not good for White.

iv) *White has no good plan*, since his pawns cannot cooperate in any aggressive action, and every good plan requires the use of pawns at some stage. This last point may not be obvious but will become clear as the game progresses.

| 17 | ♕d4 | ♘d7 |
| 18 | ♖f4 | |

White elects to act aggressively on the kingside. Black must be careful, e.g. 18...♘c5 would give White the chance to play 19 ♖af1 f6 20 ♗e4 with the idea of ♖h4 (Tiviakov). Black would then have to face an attack or play the positionally disagreeable 20...♘xe4.

| 18 | ... | ♕e7 |
| 19 | ♖af1 | ♘e5 |

Not 19...♖e8 which gives White the chance to make a favourable counter-sacrifice with 20 ♖xf7! ♕xf7 21 ♖xf7 ♔xf7 22 ♗h3 followed by 23 ♗e6+. One of White's main problems is his incapacitated bishop on g2, so Black would be very foolish to allow it onto e6.

20	♗e4	♖f8
21	♗d3	♗c8
22	♕e4	g6
23	♖f6	♔g7

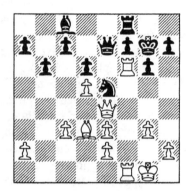

So White has done all he can. He has posted his rooks on the semi-open file; he has manoeuvred his bishop to a more active square (true, it is a target there); and he has provoked a slight weakness in Black's kingside. But now what? He needs his pawns to advance somehow to open lines for his pieces and exploit whatever chinks there are in Black's position. There are two problems with this plan:

i) The lack of good pawn advances.

ii) The absence of chinks in Black's position.

This means that, although at first glance there is nothing wrong with White's position, it has no potential. He can only wait to see if Black finds a way to strengthen *his* position. Razuvaev, however, does not want to wait, and pretends he is doing something, which only weakens his position further.

24 c4

Tiviakov suggests 24 ♕h4 or

24 ♖6f4 (with a slight advantage to Black), but such moves are easier to recommend than to play.

| 24 | ... | ♗d7 |
| 25 | h4? | |

This weakens the kingside and allows Black's next move. 25 ♕h4 or 25 ♖6f4 were still best.

| 25 | ... | ♕xf6! |
| 26 | ♖xf6 | ♔xf6 |

Now we have a different material balance (which is fully examined in another chapter). However, the nature of Black's advantage has not greatly changed. White's pawns are weak, he has no way to puncture Black's solid formation, and his bishop on d3 is an inactive, vulnerable piece. One of the greatest skills in chess is to retain an advantage in spite of simplification.

27	♕d4	♖e8
28	♔f2	♔g7
29	♔e1	f6
30	♔d2	♘g4

Provoking 31 e4 in order to further impede the bishop on d3.

| 31 | e4 | ♘e5 |
| 32 | ♕c3 | ♖e7! |

Now Tiviakov expounds his plan in schematic terms:

i) He will play his bishop to e8, his knight from d7 to c5, his rook to e5, then ...g6-g5 and ...♗g6;

ii) or his knight to f7, rook to e5, king from f8 to e7, then knight from d8 to b7 to c5, bishop to e8, ...g6-g5 and ...♗g6.

In both cases, White will lose his e-pawn without gaining obtaining any counterplay. After the demise of the e-pawn, all White's other pawns will be more vulnerable. That Black can plan so deeply and without considering White's intervening moves shows the lifeless nature of White's position.

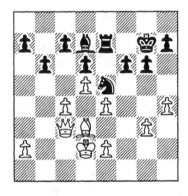

| 33 | ♕a3 | a5 |
| 34 | ♕b2 | ♘f7! |

Better than 34...♗e8 35 c5! with counterplay after 35...dxc5? 36 d6! or 35...bxc5 36 ♕b8. Now of course if 35 c5 dxc5 36 d6 ♘xd6.

35	♗c2	♖e5
36	♕a3	♔f8
37	♗a4	♗g4

Black does not want to exchange his good bishop for White's feeble cleric.

| 38 | ♕d3 | ♔e7 |
| 39 | c5? | |

White sees Black's plan gradually unfolding, and loses patience. Grandmasters know that you need counterplay, and it is not surprising that Razuvaev lashes out. Tiviakov's recommendation of 39 ♗c2 (with total

passivity) was not exactly inspiring. Black could have carried on as outlined at move 32.

39	...	dxc5
40	♕b5	♘d6
41	♕c6	♔d8
42	♗c2	

White finds his brief flourish of counterplay has faded. If 42 ♕a8+ ♗c8 and the e4 pawn is hanging. Now he must pay the price - Black's knight has been given the d6 square and Black has a passed pawn.

42	...	♗c8
43	♕a8	g5!
44	♕c6	

After 44 hxg5, Black can choose between 44...♖xg5 (winning the g3 pawn but allowing the clearance sacrifice 45 e5!?) and 44...fxg5 followed by advancing the kingside pawns to create another passed pawn.

44	...	gxh4
45	gxh4	♖h5
46	e5	

The best chance.

| 46 | ... | fxe5 |
| 47 | ♕a4 | e4 |

Cutting off the defence of the h-pawn.

| 48 | ♕b3 | ♗b7! |

Black must keep control. If 48...♖xh4 49 ♕c3! and White's queen enters on f6 or h8, harassing Black's king with checks. 48...♗b7 vacates c8 for the king, and also after the elimination of the d5 pawn, the c6 square becomes a flight square for the king. If the king can reach b7, it will be perfectly sheltered behind the queenside pawns.

49	♕c3	♗xd5
50	♕f6+	♔d7
51	a4	♔c6

Tiviakov points out that 51...♖f5 followed by 52...♖f7 was simpler. The rook is slightly misplaced on h5, which gives White some hope. However, the ultimate result of the game is not affected.

52	♕e7	♔b7
53	♔c3	♗c6
54	♔b2	c4
55	♔c3	♘c8!

An excellent move. In order to keep h4 defended, White's queen has to temporarily give up its attack on the h7 pawn. This allows Black to play ...♖c5 with gain of time.

| 56 | ♕f6 | ♖c5 |

Now Black threatens 57...h5, safeguarding his h-pawn, followed by gradual preparation of a queenside pawn advance. White's one hope is to win the h-pawn and create his own passed pawn.

| 57 | ♕h6 | ♘e7! |

Now we see another reason why 55...♘c8! was such a good move. The knight reaches d5 and White's blockade of the queenside passed pawn crumbles.

| 58 | ♕xh7 | |

The passed h-pawn is a glimmer of hope for White, but it is too late.

| 58 | ... | ♘d5+ |
| 59 | ♔d4 | |

Going backwards is no better.

59 ♔d2 e3+ 60 ♔c1 ♘f4 61 ♗d1 c3 is not clear after 62 ♕f7, but 59...c3+ 60 ♔c1 ♘b4 wins, e.g. 61 ♗xe4 c2 threatening 62...♘a2+, or 61 h5 ♖g5! followed by ...♖g1+ and ...c3-c2.

59	...	c3
60	♗xe4	♘b4
61	♗g6	♗xa4
62	h5	c2
63	♗xc2	♗xc2
64	♕f7	a4
65	h6	a3
	0-1	

Black's pawn queens with check.

We will now leave our discussion of exchange sacrifices and consider the use of pawns to shatter the opponent's centre. Here is one of the earliest known examples of such a sacrifice:

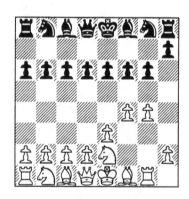

Apparently this sacrifice was played in Baghdad in the tenth century by the great Arab player *as Suli*, the leading *haliyat* or grandmaster of his time. Old rules of course apply: the queen is the weakest piece. White's opening system was in fact known as the 'torrent' pawn, since it sweeps into Black's position and wreaks destruction (or so it was hoped).

White played 1 f5! to break up Black's pawn phalanx. There followed: 1...exf5 2 gxf5 gxf5. Unfortunately for Black, bishops could only move two squares in those days, so 2...♗xf5 is not legal. However, 2...g5 keeping his pawn structure intact was better. After 2...gxf5 3 ♗h3 ♘e7 4 ♖f1 ♖f8 5 ♘g3, White regained his pawn with a clear positional advantage.

The rules of chess may have changed over the years, but the spirit of the 'torrent' pawn lives on in modern chess, as the following games demonstrate.

Karpov-Romanishin
Tilburg 1993

Black has withstood some early pressure from Karpov, and apparently has a safe game. It seems that in a few moves time the opponents will be shaking hands and agreeing a draw. White's next move, offering the exchange of queens, strengthens this impression. Unfortunately for Black, there are some hidden reefs in this position.

23 ♕a1 ♖a8?

Not suspecting any danger. Better was 23...♕xa1 24 ♖xa1 exd4 25 ♗xd4 ♖a8. White can then claim a small advantage since his bishop pair are very active. However, the a- and b-files are stripped of pawns, so Black's short-range knights are unlikely to be overstretched in their defensive task.

24 ♕xa2 ♖xa2

The rook may look impressive on this square, but it would be better on a8, defending the back rank.

25 d5 ♗b7

Equally unpleasant is 25...♗a8 26 ♖b1, and already there is a threat of 27 c5! dxc5 28 ♘c4 followed by capturing on e5, demolishing Black's centre.

26 ♖b1 (D)

26 ... ♗a6

Romanishin may have thought he could play 26...♘c5 in this position, but then 27 ♘b3! ♘xb3 (27...♘a4 28 ♗a5) 28 ♖xb3 ♖a7 29 c5 (threatening 30 c6) or 29 ♗a3!? is strong.

However, Black should have admitted that his rook on a2 is misplaced and tried 26...♖a7.

Now if 27 ♗a5 then not 27...♖xa5 28 ♖xb7 ♖c5 (defending c7) 29 ♗f1! threatening 30 ♘b3 winning, but 27...♗xd5! when all Black's problems are over. So White would have to answer 26...♖a7 with a different approach, e.g. 27 f4!? combined with c4-c5, trying to break through in the centre.

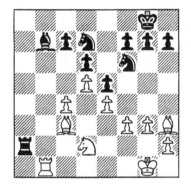

27　c5!

Now 27...♘xc5? allows mate and 27...h6 28 cxd6 cxd6 leaves Black's d-pawns vulnerable to a subsequent ♗b4. Nevertheless, this is how Black should play; after the game continuation, his centre disintegrates.

| 27 | ... | dxc5 |
| 28 | f4! | |

Completing the demolition. After 28...exf4, White can continue 29 gxf4 and his central pawn mass will quickly become overwhelming.

| 28 | ... | h5 |
| 29 | fxe5 | ♘g4 |

If 29...♘xe5 30 ♗xe5 ♖xd2 31 ♖b8+ ♔h7 32 ♗f5+ g6 (32...♔h6

33 ♗f4+) 33 ♗xf6 gxf5 34 exf5 forces mate.

| 30 | ♗xg4 | hxg4 |
| 31 | ♖a1! | |

Planning to exchange rooks, which will free his king to march up the board and capture one or more of Black's loose pawns. Romanishin has no wish to be slowly tortured by Karpov's famous technique, and throws himself on the sword.

31	...	♖c2
32	♖xa6	♖xc3
33	♖a8+	♔h7
34	e6	

The triumph of White's strategy. This pawn cannot be stopped.

34	...	fxe6
35	dxe6	♘f6
36	e7	♖c1+
37	♔f2	♖c2+
38	♔e1	1-0

If you look at the position at move 23, it is hard to believe that Black will be in serious trouble within five moves. Such is the strength of Karpov's style (and the centre-busting 27 c5!). In the following example, another seemingly solid position is fragmented by an unexpected pawn stab:

Aldama-Vera
Cuba 1993

(see following diagram)

Normally, Black's two bishops would outshine White's knights.

However, the knights have the excellent d4 square which is impregnable to pawn attack. This means they are securely centralised and defend each other in chain-like fashion. Black's queenside pawns have raced forwards in an attempt to attack White's king. Although they have forced the concession b2-b3 from White, it is Black's king, not White's, that has been left more exposed.

But how is White to exploit the Black king's lack of pawn cover? If the white queen tries to go 'round the edge' with 34 ♕h1 and 35 ♕h8, the knight on d4 is captured; and advancing pawns on the queenside would only endanger White's king. Besides, it would make no sense to attack Black directly where all his pieces are massed. If the white pawn were on g4 rather than g5, we would suggest the plan of f4-f5 to break up Black's centre. But as it is, the advance f4-f5 is impossible. Or is it? White in fact played

34   f5!!

and Black's position was suddenly hopeless. Whichever way he captures the pawn, his centre falls apart and then his king faces a massive attack. And quite right too. Black is justly punished for his neglect of the centre.

34   ...   ♗xe2

The alternatives make grim reading for Black:

a) 34...gxf5 35 g6! (the thematic undermining of the centre) 35...♗xe2 (35...♗xd4 36 g7 wins) 36 ♕xe2! ♗xd4 37 g7. Now since 37...♗xe5 38 g8(♕) defends against 38...♕g1+, Black has to try 37...axb3 38 cxb3 ♕a3 (38...♗e3 39 ♕b5+!) 39 ♕b5+ ♗b6, but now 40 ♖b8+! ♔xb8 41 ♕xb6+ and 42 g8(♕) wins.

b) 34...exf5 35 e6! ♗xe2 36 ♕xe2! ♗xd4 37 exf7 ♖xf7 (37...♗c5 38 f8(♕) ♗xf8 39 ♕b5+ ♕b6 40 ♖b8+ ♔xb8 41 ♕xb6+ ♔c8 42 ♕xg6 wins) 38 ♕b5+ ♗b6 (38...♕b6 39 ♕d5+ wins the rook) 39 ♕xd5+ ♔a6 40 ♕c4+! ♔a5 (40...♔b7 41 ♕c8 mate) 41 ♖e5+ and wins.

These variations are given to illustrate how violent the world becomes for Black's king once the centre collapses. In the game, it was by no means necessary for White to carry out such an exhaustive analysis before playing 34 f5. A little calculation would be sufficient to discover that the pawn sacrifice was very promising.

35   ♘xe2   axb3
36   axb3   exf5

Losing quickly, but 36...gxf5

37 g6 fxg6 38 ♖xe6 ♖d7 39 ♖xg6 leaves Black's king bereft of all shelter and his pawns weak and scattered.

37   ♕xd5+   ♔b6

Perhaps Black was hoping to play 38...♕a6 and 39...♖a7, but this counter-attacking idea is easily defeated by White's immediate pawn break in the centre.

38   e6   fxe6
39   ♖xe6+   ♔a5
40   ♘d4   1-0

Black resigned since 41 ♘c6+ is a winning threat, e.g. 40...♕b7 41 ♘c6+ ♔b5 42 ♕d3+ followed by 43 ♘d8+.

As a final example, we see a dramatic encounter in which White demonstrates that the question of central control can be solved by a revolutionary rather than an evolutionary approach:

Pigusov-Akopian
Novosibirsk 1993

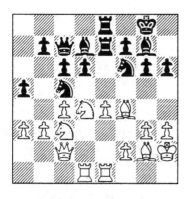

Black to move tried to ease the pressure against his d6 pawn with

22   ...   g5!?

If the bishop now retreats to c1, then 23...d5!? looks good, exploiting the pin on the e-file. Instead, Pigusov dismantled Black's centre with a tactical motif that is common in the King's Indian defence:

23   ♘db5!   cxb5
24   ♗xd6   ♕c8
25   ♗xe7   ♖xe7
26   ♘xb5

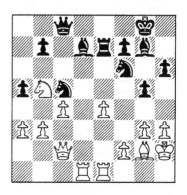

The dust has settled and White has a rook and two pawns for a knight and bishop. In a middle-game position, with all the other pieces still present, two pieces normally outweigh a rook and pawns, especially when the advantage of the bishop pair is added.

However, Black is very cramped in the game position. The knights have no safe central squares and will be dislodged by White's pawns. On being driven back, these knights will interfere with the action of Black's other pieces and stop them from functioning properly.

| 26 | ... | ♘e8? |

Black anticipates 27 e5 and voluntarily retreats his knight. The attempt to ease his cramp by exchanges also fails: 26...♗xb5 27 cxb5 (threatening b3-b4) 27...♖c7 28 b6 ♖c6 29 e5 leaves all Black's pieces hanging. But 26...♕b8! was much better. It rules out 27 e5, dissuades the plan of f4, and leaves the knight on f6 to challenge control of d5 (see White's next move). After 27 b4 axb5 28 axb4 ♗xb5 29 cxb5 ♘bd7, Black has solved his problems. So White would probably continue with 27 ♘c3 when a tense game would be in prospect.

| 27 | ♘c3! |

Now the knight is redeployed to the excellent d5 square.

| 27 | ... | a4 |

The white knight proves so strong on d5 that 27...♗xc3 was worth considering. To give up the powerful dark-squared bishop is anathema to Kings Indian players (see the section on the Indian bishop). However, the position remains unclear after 27...♗xc3 28 ♕xc3 b6 29 b4 axb4 30 axb4 ♘b7 31 f4 ♗e6, etc. In any case, the game continuation is so bad for Black that he should have tried this line.

| 28 | ♘d5! |

Not allowing Black a second chance to play ...♗xc3! (e.g. 28 b4 ♗xc3!).

| 28 | ... | ♖e6 |
| 29 | b4 | ♘b3 |

Whereas White's knight is dominant on d5, this knight becomes cut off from the action in the centre and on the kingside.

| 30 | f4! |

So that after the inevitable e5, the bishop on g7 is shut out of the game, and the knight on b3 will be further isolated (it can no longer be played to d4 under the gaze of the g7 bishop).

| 30 | ... | gxf4 |

Hopeless is 30...h5 31 e5 h4 32 f5! hxg3+ 33 ♔h1 and wherever the e6 rook goes, a fork on e7 will be fatal.

| 31 | gxf4 | ♔f8 |

Ruling out the e7 fork mentioned above, but Black's position becomes more and more constricted with every move.

| 32 | e5 | ♖c6 |
| 33 | ♕f2! |

The queen finds a way to break into Black's position. Of course, 33...♖xc4? 34 ♘b6 wins.

| 33 | ... | ♗f5 |
| 34 | c5! |

The white pawns now hold Black's pieces in a pincer-like grip.

| 34 | ... | h5 |
| 35 | ♘e3! |

The knight has done its duty on d5. Now it is necessary to clear the d-file so that White's heavy pieces can penetrate into the heart of Black's position.

| 35 | ... | ♗h6 |

The poor bishop exchanges one

blocked diagonal for another.

36   ♕h4

Threatening 37 ♖d8 ♕e6 38 ♕xh5 ♗xf4+ (what else?) 39 ♔h1 and not only is the bishop on f5 hanging, but there is also mate in two with 40 ♕h8+. Note that White was not side-tracked by the mere win of an exchange with 36

♗xc6.

36	**...**	**♖g6**
37	**♖d8**	**♖xg2+**

Desperation, but if 37...♕e6 38 ♗d5 wins (38...♕e7 39 ♘xf5).

38	**♘xg3**	**♕c7**
39	**♕f6**	**1-0**

Black resigned. His position is in ruins.

5 Sacrifices to Open Lines

When the British army in the Sudan was attacked at El Teb on 29 February 1884 by a superior force of Hadendowa tribesmen, they formed the customary 'British' square, a defensive formation of incredible strength. It consisted of one row of troops within another row, deployed as the name suggests in a square formation. As one row stood and fired, the other knelt to reload, so that continuous fire was possible. Meanwhile, a double row of bayonets presented a formidable obstacle to anyone daring to approach at close range. The British boasted that the square had never been broken.

The Hadendowa tribesmen, however, had other ideas. They concealed some warriors in a ravine, out of view of the British troops, then the main body of tribesmen attacked one side of the square. As would be expected, they were beaten off with heavy losses, and had to retreat.

The British, sensing victory, advanced in pursuit, but in moving forwards, a gap opened in the defensive line. The Hadendowa placed in ambush saw their chance and suddenly swarmed into this gap. The invincible defensive formation had been broken by a little cunning.

In chess, we also try to cajole our opponents into weakening their line of defence. We saw in the last chapter how a pawn can be used as a battering ram to break up our opponent's formation. But if the defensive line is strong, we often need a more subtle form of sacrifice: pawns must be deflected from their important function of guarding a key central square, or enticed by the lure of material gain into relinquishing the blockade of a key diagonal. Once the removal of the pawns has been achieved, our pieces - the tribesmen waiting in ambush - can seize control of the vacated squares and diagonals. This is the theme of this chapter.

I.Sokolov-Hölzl
Brünn 1991

1 d4 ♘f6 2 c4 c5 3 d5 a6 4 ♕c2

e5 5 e4 ♗d6 6 ♘c3 ♗c7 7 ♗d3
d6 8 ♘ge2 ♘h5

Played to avoid an unpleasant
pin after 9 ♗g5.

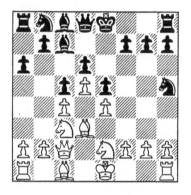

Black has shown much mis-
placed ingenuity in manoeuvring
his bishop to c7. If the position
remains closed, Black can complete his development and may
one day be able to justify his ec-
centric play. Though even in the
middlegame, the bishop would be
better on e7 (to exchange itself
for White's good bishop with
...♗g5) or fianchettoed on g7 (to
bolster a plan of ...f7-f5 attacking
White's centre). White must attempt to punish Black immediately for his faulty strategy and
neglect of development. To do so
he needs to open lines. Therefore
he began with:

9 h4!

This threatens 10 ♗g5 when
Black must play either 10...♕d7,
when the queen deprives his
knight of the natural d7 square, or
10...f6 11 ♗d2, when the knight
on h5 has its retreat cut off and is

liable to attack with f2-f3 and g2-
g4.

9 ... ♕f6

A remedy that is worse than
the disease, since now Black's
queen becomes a target. Perhaps
9...h6 was better.

10 ♗g5 ♕g6
11 ♖g1!

Black may have underesti-
mated this move. The threat is 12
g4 ♘f6 13 f4! h6 (13...exf4 14 e5
wins the queen, as does
13...♗xg4 14 f5 ♕h5 15 ♘g3) 14
f5 ♕h7 15 ♗e3 and White will
castle queenside followed by g4-
g5, suffocating Black on the
kingside.

11 ... h6
12 ♗e3 ♕f6

Black should develop with
12...♘d7 and defend doggedly,
e.g. 13 g4 ♘hf6 14 ♘f4?! ♕h7!,
though it must be admitted that
his position after the alternative
14 h5 ♕h7 15 0-0-0 ♕g8 16 ♘g3
(intending ♘f5) does not inspire
confidence.

13 0-0-0 ♘f4?

This is inexcusable reckless-
ness. Evidently, Black completely
missed White's devastating sacrifice on move 15. 13...♘d7 was
now the only chance.

14 ♘xf4 exf4
15 e5!!

An explosion which releases
all the pent-up energy in White's
position. The d3 bishop gains an
open diagonal and the knight on
c3 the lovely central e4 square.
Black now discovers why the law

of rapid development has held sway since the days of Morphy.

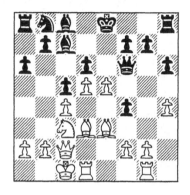

15 ... ♕xh4

Despair.

15...♕xe5 16 ♗xc5 0-0 (16...dxc5 17 ♖ge1) 17 ♗d4! ♕h5 18 g4! gives a decisive attack, e.g. 18...♕xh4 (18...♗xg4 19 f3! wins) 19 g5 h5 (19...hxg5 20 ♖h1 and 21 ♗h7+ wins) 20 ♖h1 ♕g4 21 ♖dg1 ♕d7 (21...♕f3 22 ♗e4) 22 ♖xh5 and wins.

15...dxe5 16 ♗xc5 is also hopeless, since Black can never castle, as 16...♗d6? 17 ♘e4 wins.

16 g3!

But now the g-file is opened and Black's king loses any hope of finding refuge on the kingside.

16 ... fxg3
17 ♖xg3 ♘d7

Much too late. Black is in a hopeless dilemma: if he castles kingside, he is mated; if his king stays in the centre, he also faces a massive onslaught.

18 e6 ♘e5
19 ♖xg7

If Black plays 19...fxe6, he loses the bishop on c7 (the only contribution this ill-starred piece has made to the game). But if Black does not play ...fxe6, he can never hope to develop his bishop on c8. This means that his queenside rook and bishop remain spectators as their king is hunted down.

19 ... ♔f8
20 ♖dg1 ♗d8

The bishop decides to cut short its holiday on c7, since the news from the kingside is most alarming.

21 f4

Dislodging Black's one active piece.

21 ... ♗f6

A valiant try, since after 21...♘xd3+ 22 ♕xd3 the f7 square collapses.

22 fxe5!

Its easy to be brilliant when your opponent has a rook and bishop shut out of the game.

22 ... ♗xg7
23 ♖xg7!

One can sympathise with the black bishop. After many adventures it arrives at its correct square - the one it should have gone to at move 7 or 8 - but only in time to be part of a winning combination by the opponent.

23 ... ♔xg7
24 ♕g2+ ♔f8
25 ♕f3! f6

There is no way to defend f7. If 25...♕e7 26 exd6 ♕e8 27 e7+ ♔g7 28 ♕g3+ soon mates.

26 exf6

Our familiar passed pawns. Although Black has the theoretical material advantage of two rooks for two pieces, his queenside forces remain entombed.

26   ...   ♖g8
27   ♕f4!

An elegant finishing stroke. After 27...♕xf4 28 ♗xf4, d6 can no longer be defended. Black cannot even give up a rook to stop the passed pawns, e.g. 28...♖h8 (28...♖g7 29 ♗xh6!) 29 ♗xd6+ ♔e8 30 f7+ ♔d8 31 e7+, etc.

1-0

So Black resigned. His queen's rook and bishop never even moved.

The following example is less drastic. Here, White purposefully improves his position until a dark-squared highway opens up into Black's position.

Andersson-Milos
Tilburg 1993

Apparently, Black has a safe and promising position. His knight is well anchored in the centre, and he is ready to begin an attack on White's king with ...a7-a5-a4, etc. White, on the other hand, has difficulties in attacking Black's king in view of the blocked nature of the terrain on the kingside.

However, a closer look at the position reveals that Black has some serious weaknesses on the dark squares, especially along the a1-h8 diagonal. If White could give a queen check on this diagonal, it would be mate. Likewise, if a knight could get to f7. The black knight on e4 is also not as securely placed as may appear at first glance, and can be undermined.

All these considerations suggest White's correct plan: he must stage a breakthrough in the centre which both dislodges Black's knight and gains access for the queen to the key dark-square diagonal leading to Black's king. Andersson's play shows us how this is done.

20   ♘d2!   ♘d6

The knight voluntarily retreats, anticipating White's next move. Note that 20...♘c3+ 21 bxc3 bxc3+ 22 ♘b3 followed by ♕xc3 is not dangerous for White.

21   f3   c5
22   dxc5   ♘xc5
23   e4

Carrying out his plan. Black tries to block the position and prevent the fragmentation of his centre.

23	...	dxe4
24	fxe4	f4
25	e5	♘xd3

If 25...♘f5 26 e6! is strong, e.g. 26...♕xe6 27 ♗xf5 ♕xf5 28 ♕xe7 or 26...♘e3 27 ♘c4 ♘xc4 28 ♗xc4, and again Black has to worry about sudden death on the a1-h8 diagonal.

| 26 | ♘xd3 | ♘f5 |

Black may have been feeling very pleased with himself in this position. He has only to play 27...♗e6 and the troublesome a1-h8 diagonal will be cleared forever. Then he can continue his own attack on White's king beginning with moves such as ...♘e3 and ...♖gc8, and would have good chances of success. However, White frustrated all Black's hopes with a thematic pawn sacrifice:

| 27 | e6! |

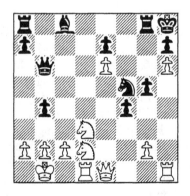

| 27 | ... | ♕xe6 |

If 27...♘e3 28 ♘f1! ♗xe6 (the knight dare not move) 29 ♘xe3

fxe3 (29...♕xe3 30 ♕xb4) 30 ♕g3 and White has dangerous attacking chances.

However, Black could have tried 27...♕e3. The black queen swoops into the centre and challenges White's queen. Best play is then 28 ♘c4 (28 ♕f1 ♘g3) 28...♕xe1 29 ♖dxe1 and White has a clear advantage, e.g. 29...a5 30 ♘b6 ♖b8 31 ♘xc8 ♖bxc8 32 ♘e5 ♘d6 33 ♘f7+ or 29...♖b8 30 ♘ce5 ♗xe6? 31 ♘c6. If Black attempts to improve his king position, then simply ♘xb4 will give White a good endgame.

It is notable that when Black deals adequately with one mating theme - a queen check on the a1-h8 diagonal - he is brought down by the secondary mating theme of ♘e5-f7.

| 28 | ♘e4 | ♖b8 |

Not 28...♗b7 29 ♘dc5 followed by 30 ♕xb4. 29 ♘xg5!? may also be strong.

| 29 | ♘xb4 | ♖b5 |

This leaves the back rank weakened, allowing White a winning combination. However, there was no other good defence against the threat of 30 ♕c3+.

| 30 | ♕c3+ | ♕e5 |
| 31 | ♘xg5! |

Now Black's position collapses in a few moves.

31...♖xg5 32 ♖d8+ ♖g8 33 ♖xg8+ ♔xg8 34 ♕xc8+ ♔f7 35 ♕c4+ e6 36 ♘d3 ♕b8 37 ♖e1 ♖b6 38 b3

Here Black overstepped the time limit. He is of course quite lost - he is already a pawn down and the f-pawn is also dropping, to say nothing of his exposed king.

Note how all sorts of tactical possibilities appeared for White after the sacrifice 27 e6!. Here is a similar example:

Rodriguez-Sorin
Matanzas 1993

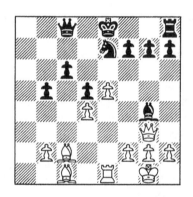

Black tried

21	...	♘g6

and was struck down by

22	e6!	

that move again!

22	...	♗xe6
23	h4!	

There is no defence against the threat of 24 h5 followed by, after the knight retreats, 25 ♕xg7, decimating Black's kingside. Black cannot even escape the worst by sacrificing the exchange, since 23...0-0 24 h5 ♘e7 25 ♗h6 g6 26 ♕e5! wins a piece. So in the game, he played

23	...	♔d7

but not surprisingly his king proved fatally exposed:

24	h5	♘e7
25	♕xg7	♖g8
26	♕f6	♕e8
27	♗g5!	

This threatens 28 ♖a1 followed by 29 ♖a7 winning. Hence Black's desperate reply.

27	...	h6
28	♗xh6	

Or 28 ♗h4 followed by 29 ♖a1.

28	...	♖g4
29	♗f4	♕g8
30	g3	♕a8
31	♕e5	♕a5
32	h6	1-0

The pawn queens.

Let us return to the diagram position above. Imagine if after 21...♘g6, White had played an inconsequential move, for example 22 ♔h1, instead of 22 e6. Then Black could play 22...♗f5! eliminating White's powerful light-squared bishop, followed by ...0-0 with a safe game. So clearly after 21...♘g6, White must act fast, since 22...♗f5 is a strong positional threat. That is why he played 22 e6! to rule out 22...♗f5 - the bishop is pinned along the e-file after 22...♗xe6. Also, White gained time after 22...♗xe6 23 h4 to threaten 24 h5, since with the bishop no longer on g4, the white queen's route to g7 is unobstructed and there is no option of ...♗xh5.

21...♘g6 therefore failed to

solve Black's problems. Perhaps he should simply have castled? Then 21...0-0 22 e6 ♗xe6 is nothing. Or if 22 ♗xh7+ ♔xh7 23 ♕h4+ ♔g8 24 ♕xe7 ♕e6 and the presence of opposite-coloured bishops makes White's winning task very difficult, despite his extra pawn. However, White can play 22 ♗g5 ♘g6 23 ♕d3! to stop Black exchanging the light-squared bishops. Now he is ready to retreat his bishop from g5 and begin a general central/kingside advance beginning with f2-f4 and f4-f5, etc. In view of White's strong bishops and superior pawn structure, Black would face an arduous defensive task. From these variations, a general conclusion can be drawn about the position: if Black is to equalise, he must exchange light-squared bishops without being immediately punished.

So why not play 21...♗f5 immediately, in order to challenge White's good bishop? This looks good, since 22 ♗xf5 ♘xf5 followed by ...0-0 is best avoided by White. However, White can still try the pawn sacrifice 21...♗f5 22 e6!? *(D)*.

Now Black is best advised not to take the bishop: 22...♗xc2 23 ♕xg7 ♖f8 24 ♗h6 ♘g6 25 e7 ♖h8 26 ♕f8+!! and wins.

Taking the pawn is also fraught with danger: 22...fxe6 (22...♗xe6 23 ♕xg7 ♖g8 24 ♕xh7 is totally bad) 23 ♗g5! ♗xc2 (23...0-0 24 ♗xe7 or 23...♕b7 24 ♗xe7 ♗xc2

25 ♕xg7 wins) 24 ♗xe7 ♔xe7 (if 24...♗g6 25 ♗c5 leaves Black unable to castle and facing the threat of ♖a1-a7 combined with ♕d6) 25 ♕xg7+ ♔d6 26 ♖a1 ♗a4 (else 27 ♖a7 follows, with threat of mate on e5 or e7, e.g. 26...♖g8 27 ♕e5+ ♔d7 28 ♖a7+ ♔e8 29 ♕d6 ♕d8 30 ♕xe6+ and mate on f7) 27 b3! and White regains his piece with a winning attack on Black's king, or after 27...♗xb3 wins as in the bracketed note above after 28 ♕e5+.

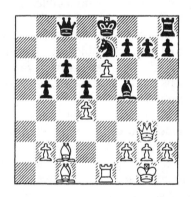

(analysis diagram)

However, there is a third option: 22...0-0! and Black escapes punishment, e.g. 23 ♗g5 ♗xc2 24 ♗xe7 ♖e8 25 ♗f6 (25 exf7+ ♔xf7 26 ♕f4+ ♕f5) 25...♗g6 26 exf7+ ♔xf7 27 ♖xe8 ♕xe8.

But finally, after 21...♗f5, White can play 22 ♕xg7 ♖g8 23 ♗xf5! ♕xf5 24 ♕f6 with an extra pawn, instead of 22 e6!?. It is not always best to sacrifice!

By now, the reader will be aware that even the simplest or

the most positional of sacrifices often requires long and detailed tactical calculation. But in truth, this complexity applies to any manoeuvre on the chessboard, not just a sacrificial one. Chess is a very complicated game, and every position has to be adjudged on its unique features. We should rejoice in this, since otherwise chess would have succumbed to the 'draw death' predicted in the 1920s. Anyone who had mastered the laws of strategy to a high degree would be invincible. Botvinnik, despite his venerable age, would still be world champion (even if incapable of scoring more than a draw against young rivals such as Fischer or Kasparov)!

Fortunately, chess has remained too complex for even the brightest minds to fully master. Here is a good example of a modern struggle between two young players who undoubtedly understand chess strategy. Their play is full of invention and finesse - but chess perfection is not granted to man!

Kamsky-Bareev
Biel 1993

(see following diagram)

Here White played
18   f5!
with the following ideas:

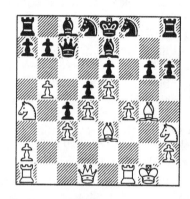

a) If Black plays 18...gxf5, then 19 ♗h5+ and now 19...♘f7 20 ♗xf7+ ♔xf7 21 ♕h5+ leads to a mating attack after 21...♔g7 22 ♔h1 followed by ♖g1+; or if 21...♘g6 then 22 ♘f4 ♖g8 23 ♔h1 followed by ♖g1, winning the pinned knight. (Kamsky probably only calculated as far as 21 ♕h5+ ♔g7 22 ♔h1. His judgement told him there *must* be a win with Black's king in such an exposed position.) So Black must play 19...♔d7.

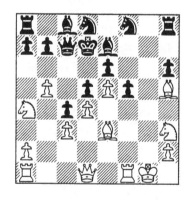

(analysis diagram)

White has no immediate win here, but Black's pieces are hopelessly unco-ordinated. His king on d7 boxes in the bishop on c8, which in turn shuts the queens rook out of the game. The knight on d8 has no safe move, and merely takes away the d8 square from the king. This prevents an 'unwinding' with ...♔d8, followed by ...♗d7, ...♖e8 and ...♘f7.

Black therefore has no constructive plan after 19...♔d7. Meanwhile, White can strengthen his position move by move. This is a key feature of a good positional sacrifice. Although the position at first glance may seem fairly equal, one side is playing with a plan, while the other is floundering around wondering what to do. He can merely respond to direct threats and not undertake any direct campaign.

Thus, after 19...♔d7, White can plan an invasion along the g-file, beginning with 20 ♔h1 followed by doubling rooks on the g-file. If Black tries to contest control of the g-file with his own rook on h8, by say 20...♖g8, then White can simply exchange it off by 21 ♖g1, when he will be able to bring up reinforcements, i.e. the rook on a1, while Black's own reserves are entombed on the queenside. A sample variation: 20 ♔h1 b6 (Black must try to develop somehow) 21 ♖g1 a6 22 bxa6 ♗xa6 23 ♖g7 ♗b5 24 ♕g1 (threatening 25 ♖xe7+!) 24...♖h7 (if 24...♔c8 25 ♘xb6+! ♕xb6 26

♖xe7 wins) 25 ♖xh7 ♘xh7 26 ♘b2 ♔c8 27 ♗xh6 ♘f8 28 a4 ♗a6 (28...♗d7 29 ♕g8) 29 ♕g8 ♘d7 30 ♘f4 ♕c6 31 ♕e8! ♗h4 32 ♘g2 and wins.

Alternatively, White could plan a further sacrifice after 19...♔d7 to destroy Black's centre and mate his king. This would begin with ♘f4 and ♕f3, followed by ♘xd5. White, however, should not be in a hurry to play ♘xd5 since, as stated above, Black can do little to improve his position. So for example White could play ♖ad1 (after ♕f3 of course) so that the rook would be on a generally superior square once ♘xd5 was played.

But as a general rule, you should not risk a sacrifice when you have a clear, simple winning method. In the position after 19...♔d7, Black is defenceless against White's plan of penetration down the g-file. Therefore unless everything has been carefully worked out, so that the ♘xd5 breakthrough is merely a technical device and not a true sacrifice, the gradual approach with ♔h1 and ♖g1 is to be preferred. Now we will return to the position after 18 f5!.

b) Bareev in the game answered with

18 ... exf5

He may well have rejected 18...gxf5 19 ♗h5+ ♔d7 as an option purely on intuitive grounds. As the readers experience grows, he or she too will learn to make instant judgements such as 'Oh, 18...gxf5 19 ♗h5+ ♔d7 looks terrible - it's not even worth looking at.' A well-developed positional sense is a must for any strong player, since it saves valuable time and energy which would otherwise be spent looking at 'rubbish'. Though of course there is one drawback: there may occasionally be a diamond in amongst the rubbish!

The game continued:

19   ♗f3

Now imagine that Black's b-pawn were on b6 in this position. Then Black could play 19...♗b7 20 ♘f4 ♕d7 followed by ...♘de6 and ...0-0-0. Black's pieces would be excellently co-ordinated and he would be a pawn up. White would have great difficulty in drawing the game. Instead, the pawn is on b7, and Bareev could find nothing better than

19   ...   ♗e6

to defend his e-pawn. But now he cannot utilise the e6 square for one of his knights, and the bishop proves vulnerable to attack on e6 after ♘f4 or ♘c5. White has good play for his pawn. In other words, altering the position ever so slightly, by putting a black pawn on b6 rather than b7, turns the exclamation mark after 18 f5 into a question mark. That is why every position has to be carefully examined and handled according to its specific features. 18 f5! is an excellent concept and well worth adding to the reader's rep-

ertoire of ideas. However, he should not imagine that the next time he reaches a similar position in a game that such a sacrifice *must* be the correct strategy.

20   ♘f4   ♗g5

Black defends against the threat to his d-pawn by tactical means. 21 ♗xd5? ♗xf4 or 21 ♘xd5? ♗xd5 22 ♗xg5 ♗xf3 23 ♗xd8 ♗xd1 24 ♗xc7 ♗xa4 lose a piece.

21   ♘c5

But now that Black's bishop has duties on g5, a gap has opened up for White's other knight. We begin to see the compensation that White has gained for his pawn. Both knights, which were passively place on the side of the board, have found a new freedom: one in a direct way through the vacating of the f4 square, the other indirectly through the cumulative effect of White's pressure. Of course, the target is the d5 pawn and its defenders. Now for example, there really is a threat of 22 ♘xd5 since the knight on a4 no longer hangs after 21...♗g8 22 ♘xd5 ♗xd5 23 ♗xg5 ♗xf3 24 ♗xd8 ♗xd1 25 ♗xc7. Therefore Black is obliged to capture the knight.

21   ...   ♗xf4
22   ♗xf4   ♕e7

The only answer to the threat of ♘xe6 and ♗xd5.

23   ♕e2

Methodical play, preparing ♕g2.

23   ...   ♘f7

Clearing d8 so the rook can defend the d-pawn.

24   a4!

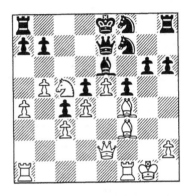

Another useful strengthening of his position. Now Bareev gives 24...g5 25 ♗c1 ♘g6 as 'unclear'. However, 26 ♗h5! is clearly to White's advantage, e.g. 26...♘f4 27 ♗xf4 gxf4 28 ♘xe6 followed by ♖xf4 and the f5 pawn is doomed; or 26...♖g8 27 ♗xg6 ♖xg6 28 ♕c2! ♗c8 (in fact it's better to allow White to play ♘xe6 and ♕xf5, recovering the pawn with a big advantage) 29 ♗a3!

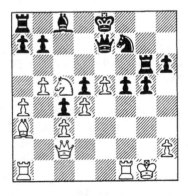

(analysis diagram)

White has a crushing attack, e.g. 29...♕c7 (getting out of any discovered attack by White's knight) 30 ♖xf5! ♗xf5 31 ♕xf5 ♖g8 (31...♖g7 32 ♘e6) 32 ♖f1 ♘d8 (32...♖c8 33 ♕e6+ wins) 33 ♘d7! ♕xd7 34 ♕f8+ ♖xf8 35 ♖xf8 mate.

The value of 24 a4 is apparent in this variation: if the pawn were still on a2, 29 ♗a3? could be answered by 29...b6! winning a piece; but with 24 a4, the bishop is defended by the rook. Thus, 29...b6 can be answered by 30 ♘e4 ♕c7 31 ♘f6+ ♔d8 32 ♘xd5 winning. I'm sure Kamsky did not calculate this variation when he played 24 a4; but he probably did consider in general terms the idea of ♗c1-a3 or the advance a4-a5-a6 followed by ♘b7 and ♘d6+. Its not surprising that favourable variations appear 'naturally' from a well thought out positional build up.

Bareev however rises to the occasion and finds the correct defensive plan, a plan he curiously criticises in his own notes to the game!

24   ...   ♘g5!

Black plans to eliminate the bishop which is the persecutor of the d-pawn, or at least blockade its action through entrenching the knight on e4. Kamsky does not allow this and removes the knight, but at the cost of making the plan of ♗c1 and ♗a3 impossible.

25   ♗xg5   hxg5!

If 25...♛xg5+ 26 ♔h1 ♛e7 (the only answer to the twin threats of ♘xe6 and ♘xb7) 27 ♛g2 ♖d8 28 a5 keeps up the pressure. There is a strong threat of 29 a6 b6 30 ♘d7! followed by 31 ♘d6+ winning the d-pawn. After 25...hxg5, Black has activated his king's rook and hopes for counterplay against h2.

26 ♘xe6

Another advantage of 25...hxg5 is seen in the variation 26 ♛g2 ♖d8 27 a5 g4! forcing the bishop away from the attacking diagonal. Kamsky's move wins back the pawn.

26	...	♛xe6
27	♛g2	0-0-0
28	♛xg5	♘h7
29	♛g2	

Material equality has been restored, and White is a little better. Black's queen and queens rook are tied to the defence of the d-pawn, and the passed e-pawn is a permanent long-term advantage for White.

But where is White to make progress? Not on the queenside, since Black can always ensure it stays unopened. For example, if White plays a4-a5 and a5-a6, Black replies ...b7-b6; or if a4-a5 and b5-b6, then ...a7-a6 by Black and again the queenside is blocked. White may try to force a favourable closure of the queenside, but the actual breakthrough must come elsewhere.

The centre is blocked, and will remain so, unless White achieves the unlikely advance e5-e6. Therefore, all White's hopes of a winning breakthrough rest on the kingside. First, he has to try to force a weakness in Black's pawn structure f5/g6. This will be very difficult to achieve, since if White plays ♔h1 and ♖g1, Black can simply play ...♖g8 defending the g-pawn. And it is impractical to use the h-pawn as a battering ram to break up Black's pawns. White's king would be left too exposed.

Therefore, White has no realistic way to improve his position. So a draw seems the natural result. But it is not so easy for Black, and Bareev plays the very move that White wants to provoke:

29 ... g5?

The intention is noble: 30...g4 and 31...♘g5-e4, putting the knight on a gigantic central square. Unfortunately, Kamsky can prevent this plan, and the weakness of the pawns remains. Probably best was 29...♔b8.

30 &d1!

This threatens 31 ♖xf5!, which also answers 30...g4. It also prepares &c2, pressurising the f-pawn. Sooner or later, Black will be obliged to play ...f5-f4, and then further ways for White to strengthen his position will become clear.

30 ... ♔b8
31 &c2 f4

Note that the f-pawn is far more vulnerable to attack than the d5 pawn, since frontal pressure can be applied by White's rooks. Now White has a logical plan to exploit the weaknesses in Black's kingside:

i) Double rooks on the f-file, which will blunt any attempt by Black to start a kingside attack with ...g5-g4 and ...g4-g3.

ii) Play the bishop to g4, and chase the queen from e6.

iii) Then advance e5-e6! at an appropriate moment followed by ♖e1 and ♖e5.

iv) And finally win the d-pawn or g-pawn through the combined pressure of rook, bishop and queen.

It is now clear that Black's kingside pawns had two blockading functions. Not only was it their 'duty' to form a barrier to White's rooks, but they were also required to shut out the white bishop from control of e6. They have failed in the second of these tasks. This in turn means that Black's queen will be driven from e6, and that the whole

blockade will eventually crumble.

32 ♖f2 ♖dg8
33 ♖af1 ♘f8?

A blunder, which should accelerate the end. 33...♖d8 was best, but Black would have no answer in the long term to White's strategy outlined above.

34 &d1!

The bishop now comes to g4 with even greater force. Black must lose the d-pawn, for example: 34...♘g6 35 &g4 and e5-e6, or 34...♘h7 35 &f3 ♖d7 36 &g4 (Bareev).

34 ... ♘h7
35 &g4 ♕f7
36 a5?

Simply 36 e6 wins the d-pawn, e.g. 36...♕c7 37 ♕xd5 ♘f6 38 ♕f5!; Kamsky may have been put off by 38 ♕g2? ♖xh2!! when 39 ♔xh2? f3+ wins the queen.

36 ... ♖d8

A respite for Black, but his position remains unpleasant.

37 b6 a6
38 ♖e1!

Since White did not take advantage of Black's blunder at move 33, the game continues in the pattern outlined at move 31. 38 ♖e1 begins part (iii).

38 ... ♕e7
39 &f5 ♘f6

Black cannot prevent White from carrying out his plan. Here, as Bareev points out, White should play 40 ♖fe2 ♘e8 41 e6. Sooner or later, White can win the d-pawn with ♖e5 and &g4-f3. Instead, in time pressure, White played

40   ♖ef1?

and agreed to a draw. Black can try 40...♘h5 aiming to get his knight to e6, e.g. 41 ♖e1 (correcting his mistake) 41...♘g7 42 ♗g4 ♘e6. Black has blocked the hole in his position. White could try 40...♘h5 41 e6!? ♘g7 42 ♕g4 ♘xe6 43 ♖e1 ♖h6 44 ♖fe2 ♖d6, but Black can probably weather the storm.

Although strong players nowadays are aware of all the standard tactical devices, a sacrifice can still surprise even the most battle-hardened grandmaster. Yuri Razuvaev is one of the most solid of all Russian grandmasters. He was selected to play board 8 in the USSR-Rest of the World match in London in 1984, ahead of many illustrious Soviet grandmasters, since he could draw with anyone. He duly obliged - four draws against Hübner! Yet for all his experience, in the following game he misses a strong sacrifice that costs him the game.

Kindermann-Razuvaev
Prague 1992

A tense position. White has control of the e-file and a more compact pawn structure around his king. Black on the other hand is exerting enormous pressure against the g2 square both diagonally and frontally. Razuvaev played:

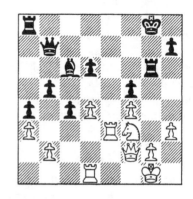

31   ...   h6

His idea is to continue 32...♗e4, blocking the e-file, and then 33...♔h7 followed by 34...♖ag8, bringing all his pieces to bear against g2. If g2 drops, then White's position will collapse. Black played 31...h6 first so that after ...♗e4 he is not troubled by ♘g5. However, he had overlooked White's next move, which crosses his plan and leaves him in a wretched position. He should have played 31...♗e4 immediately when, after 32 ♘g5 d5 33 ♘xe4 fxe4, an interesting position is reached in which Black has the superior long-term pawn structure (a protected passed pawn on e4) but his king is somewhat exposed. Evidently, Razuvaev was looking for a more advantageous outcome to the struggle, but he overestimated his position.

32   d5!   ♗xd5

Of course, if Black had played 31...♗e4 last move, he could simply ignore 32 d5 and play

32...h6.

33	♘h4!	♖g7
34	♖g3	

Now White's compensation for the pawn sacrifice becomes clear. The square d4 has been vacated, so White is threatening 35 ♖xg7+ ♔xg7 (35...♕xg7 36 ♖xd5) 36 ♕d4+ winning a piece. Meanwhile, 35 ♘xf5 is also threatened, when Black's kingside is ripped apart.

34	...	♗e4

The only move. If White's d-pawn were still on d4, White's attack would now be at an end. But as it is, his queen's rook makes a powerful entrance, at the same time restoring material equality.

35	♖xd6	

Yes. 32 d5! was a good move. Ask White's queen's rook!

35	...	♔h7

Or the h-pawn would be taken as well. White is now dominant on the dark squares, which allow him to penetrate into Black's position.

36	♖xg7+	♕xg7
37	♕b6!	

Threatening 38 ♖g6 ♕f8 39 ♕c7+ ♔h8 40 ♖g3! followed by 41 ♘g6+.

37	...	♕a7

Managing to exchange queens and thereby avoid the direct attack, but at the price of a losing endgame.

38 ♖xh6+ ♔g7 39 ♖g6+ ♔f7 (39...♔h7 40 ♖d6) 40 ♖f6+ ♔g7 41 ♘xf5+ ♗xf5 42 ♕xa7+ ♖xa7

43 ♖xf5 b4 44 ♖b5 bxa3 45 bxa3 ♖f7 46 g3 ♖c7 47 ♖b2 ♖d7 48 ♔f2 c3 49 ♖e2 ♔f6 50 ♔e3 1-0

In the next example, Black can be forgiven for missing White's clever idea:

Sherbakov-Karlsson
Täby 1991

1 d4 e6 2 c4 f5 3 ♘c3 ♘f6 4 ♘f3 ♗b4 5 ♗g5 0-0 6 ♖c1 d6 7 g3 ♘bd7 8 ♗g2 ♕e8 9 ♗xf6 ♘xf6 10 0-0 ♗xc3 11 ♖xc3 e5 12 dxe5 dxe5

13	e4!!	

An incredible move, giving up the e-pawn 'for nothing'.

13	...	♘xe4

It is hard to refuse such a gift, but 13...f4! was better, when White's bishop remains shut out of the game. However, this is only apparent in hindsight.

14	♖e3	c6

Ruling out 15 ♕d5+ winning

the e-pawn. How is White to continue his attack now?

15 b3!!

This is White's idea. He will play 16 ♕a1 and win back the e-pawn. Note that if White re-establishes material equality, he will have a good game: the black knight can easily be ousted from e4, and the weakness in Black's centre caused by ...f7-f5 will remain. Karlsson is not so obliging, however.

15	...	♕e7
16	♕a1	♖e8
17	♖fe1	♕c5

After 17...♗d7 18 ♘h4 followed by 19 ♘xf5 and 20 ♗xe4, White has regained his pawn and e5 is kept terminally weak (18...g6? 19 f3 or 18...♘f6 19 ♖xe5 are both unsatisfactory for Black). So Black sets a crafty trap. If 18 ♘h4 then 18...♘xf2! and 19 ♔xf2? f4 or 19 fxe5?? ♘h3+ both lose for White. After 19 b4! ♕xb4 20 ♔xf2 e4 followed by ...♗e6, Black has three pawns and dynamic play for his piece. Sherbakov finds a simple way to keep control:

18 ♕b2!

Defending f2. Now the plan of ♘h4 leads to a positional advantage and no complications.

18	...	a5
19	♘h4	♕d4
20	♕c2	a4

After 20...♘d6, the retreat 21 ♘f3 is simple and strong.

21 ♘xf5

At last. Eight moves after sac-

rificing his pawn, White regains it and eventually receives the e5 pawn as interest.

21	...	♗xf5
22	♗xe4	axb3
23	axb3	♗xe4
24	♖xe4	♖a1
25	♖xa1	♕xa1+
26	♔g2	♖f8
27	♕e2	♕b1

27...♖e8 28 f4 wins the e-pawn, and 27...♖f5 28 f4 exf4? 29 ♖e8+ leads to mate.

28 ♖xe5 h6

Black finds to his consternation that he is mated after 28...♕xb3 29 ♖e8 ♕b4 30 ♕e6+ ♔h8 31 ♕f7!. Therefore he cannot regain his pawn.

| 29 | ♕e3 | ♖d8 |
| 30 | ♖e7 | ♖d1 |

A desperate counter-attack that accelerates the end.

31	♕e6+	♔h7
32	♖e8	♖g1+
33	♔h3	1-0

Black is soon mated after 33...♕f1+ 34 ♔h4 g5+ 35 ♔h5 ♕d1+ 36 g4.

Tarrasch once wryly remarked 'Chess is a terrible game. If you have no centre, your opponent has a freer position. If you do have a centre, then you really have something to worry about!' The Australian grandmaster Rogers finds himself trapped in this paradox in the next game. He builds a centre in order to deprive his opponent's pieces of open lines, only to find it decimated by some flanking blows from White's restricted army.

Rosentalis-Rogers
Mälmo 1993

---

1 e4 c5 2 c3 ♘f6 3 e5 ♘d5 4 g3 d6 5 exd6 e6 6 ♗g2 ♗xd6 7 ♘f3 ♘c6 8 0-0 0-0 9 ♘a3 ♗e7 10 d3 b6 11 ♘c4 ♗b7 12 a4 ♕c7 13 ♕e2 ♖ad8 14 ♗d2 ♖fe8 15 ♖ae1 ♗f8

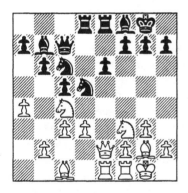

Both sides have played the opening somewhat cautiously and are now well entrenched behind their own lines. White's next move provokes Black into advancing his centre pawns.

16 ♗g5 f6
17 ♗c1 e5

Now White can claim that Black has loosened his pawn front, while Black can point to his space advantage in the centre.

18 ♘h4

With the idea of an eventual f4, undermining Black's centre. The knight itself may also move to f5;

when it is kicked out by ...g7-g6, a slight weakness appears in Black's kingside.

18 ... ♕d7

Stopping ♘f5 and also with designs against the d3 pawn. A good alternative was 18...♗c8! redeploying the bishop to e6 where it strengthens Black's influence on white squares such as e6, f7 and f5 which have been neglected by the pawn advances ...f7-f6 and ...e6-e5.

19 ♕c2

With vague ideas of 20 ♗e4 and 21 d4!? attacking h7. The queen also moves from the e-file in preparation for f4.

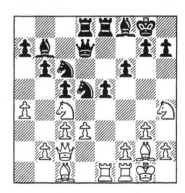

19 ... g5?

One pawn advance too many. Black could have countered the idea of 20 ♗e4 with 19...♘ce7!, then 20 ♗e4 g6 21 ♘g2 (preparing f2-f4) 21...f5! 22 ♘xe5 (22 ♗f3 ♘b4!) 22...♕c7 23 ♗f3 ♗g7 24 ♘c4 ♘b4! 25 cxb4 (25 ♕d1 ♖xd3) 25...♗xf3 gives Black excellent play for the pawn. The light-squared bishop is so menacing to White's king that he will have great difficulty surviving an attack after ...♞c6-d4 or ...♛c6 and ...♞d5.

White of course can (and should) avoid this variation, say with 20 ♞f3, but he is making no progress at all. After 19...g5, on the other hand, he has a clear target, the flimsy e5/f6/g5 structure, which is ripe for demolition with a timely f2-f4.

20 ♞f3 ♞c7
21 ♞fd2!?

White decides that firm measures are called for, and so he sacrifices his d-pawn to speed up his attack on Black's centre. The conservative 21 ♖d1 is ineffectual, since after 21...♞e6, the advance d3-d4 is hard to achieve and White is therefore left without a plan.

21 ... ♛xd3!

White may have some useful positional trumps after this move, but a pawn is always a pawn. We have seen some beautiful examples of sacrificial play in this book, but it should never be forgotten that (to misquote Tartakower) it is normally better to sacrifice the *opponent's* pieces.

22 ♛xd3 ♖xd3
23 ♞e4 ♚g7

Not 23...♝g7 24 Ned6 ♖b8 25 ♞xb7 and wins the knight on c6.

24 f4!

Finally, White has achieved the long desired advance. Black has an extra pawn, but White has more than adequate compensa-

tion:

i) The potential pressure which White's bishop on g2 exerts along the diagonal h1-a8 is very unpleasant for Black. This pressure becomes important in a number of variations; for example, see the note at move 23. Put the black bishop on a8, a defended square, and Black's defensive task is eased. Black however is never allowed the luxury of a free tempo to play ...♝a8 in the game.

ii) White's last move dynamites Black's fragile kingside pawn structure. Despite the exchange of queens, the position still has the character of a middlegame rather than an endgame: all the other pieces are still present. This means that king safety is still a priority. After the black bulwark e5/f6/g5 is dissolved, Black will face an attack from all White's pieces. Most of Black's minor pieces, on the other hand, are on the queenside and cannot easily return to the defence of the king. (This is another reason why the bishop on g2 is doing such an excellent job: it pins down pieces which would otherwise rush to the kingside.)

iii) White has a clear plan of attack and the means to carry out this plan. Black, on the other hand, has an onerous defensive task and can only respond to one move threats.

Obviously, Rogers did not relish defending his position and fails to find the line which minimises White's advantage.

| 24 | ... | exf4 |
| 25 | gxf4 | h6? |

Black should play 25...g4! returning the extra pawn to keep the kingside blocked. Then after 26 ♘f2 ♖dd8 27 ♘xg4 ♗a8! (Black now has the free tempo needed for this useful move) 28 ♘ce3 ♘e7! (defending f5) Black has almost equalised. Rogers holds on to his extra pawn, but seems to forget that it is still possible to be mated by a direct attack even after the queens have been exchanged.

| 26 | fxg5 | fxg5 |
| 27 | h4! | |

The next stage in the destruction of Black's kingside.

27	...	gxh4
28	♖f6! *(D)*	
28	...	♘d8

Rosentalis points out that 28...♖xe4, hoping for 29 ♗xe4 ♖g3+ winning a piece, loses out to 29 ♖g6+!! and White wins. We repeat: you can only play suc-

cessful positional chess if you have a sharp eye for tactics.

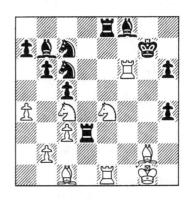

It seems that Black has no good moves after 28 ♖f6. Alternatives to 28...♘d8 are no better: 28...h3!? 29 ♗h1! (better than 29 ♗f1 ♖g3+ 30 ♘xg3 ♔xf6!) 29...♖g3+ 30 ♔f2 ♖g6 31 ♖xg6+ ♔xg6 32 ♖g1+ and wins the exchange by a knight fork on d6 or f6. If instead 29...♗e7 then 30 ♗xh6+ ♔g8 31 ♔h2 and 32 ♖g1+ is a winning threat since 31...♗xf6 32 ♘xf6+ ♔f7 33 ♘xe8 ♘xe8 34 ♗xc6 ♗xc6 25 ♘e5+ wins.

Alternatively, Black could try 28...♗e7 but 29 ♗xh6+ ♔g8 30 ♖ef1 ♗xf6 31 ♘xf6+ ♔f7 32 ♘d5+ ♔g6 33 ♖f6+ ♔h5 34 ♘f4+ ♔g4 35 ♘xd3 wins.

29	♗xh6+	♔g8
30	♗xf8	♖xf8
31	♖g6+	♔h8
32	♘e5	

Now a deadly swarm of white pieces descend on Black's king.

| 32 | ... | ♖d5 |
| 33 | ♘g5 | ♖f5 |

The rook on d5 cannot retreat: 33...♖d2 34 ♗xb7 ♘xb7 35 ♘ef7+ wins. So White's pressure on the long diagonal finally wins the exchange.

34　♗xd5　♗xd5
35　c4!　♗a8
36　♖d1　1-0

If the knight on d8 moves, 37 ♘ef7+ wins, and 36...♖e8 is met by 37 ♖xd8.

The reader should not imagine that only pawns can effect a breakthrough, although they are of course the most common sacrificial choice - a plentiful and cheap supply of cannon fodder. Next we see how Kamsky solves the problem of penetrating a well-entrenched and apparently invincible defensive line.

Kamsky-Yusupov
Linares 1993

White is the exchange up, and at first glance seems to have an easy win. But how *exactly* is he to break through? There is only one

semi-open file on the queenside. If White doubles rooks on the b-file, Black simply plays ...♗c6 (not however ...b7-b6? which would expose the pawns to attack after a3-a4-a5). The situation is almost as blocked on the king-side. The knight on f7, which shields the f-file, also keeps the rook out of h8.

The knight evidently holds together Black's position. So why not eliminate it with 33 ♘xg5? The problem is that 33...♘xg5 34 ♖xg5 g6! leaves the rook trapped on g5. If 35 ♖f1 ♔g7 36 ♖f6 ♗f7 (but not 36...♔h6? 37 ♖h5+) and the bishop moves between f7 and e8 until White agrees a draw, or Black can try ...♖c7-c6-a6 and attack the a-pawn.

In such a blocked position, a knight can be a more useful piece than a rook. A rook must stop when it reaches a brick wall; a knight can leap over it. Therefore, White must find a favourable moment to play ♖xg5!, returning the exchange but remaining with an agile knight against a slightly restricted bishop. However, it is hard to imagine that White can win against good defensive play.

33　♖bh1

Kamsky decides his best practical winning chance is to probe the position. Perhaps he will discover a way to win, or maybe Black will lose patience and weaken himself somehow.

33　...　♖c7!

Here for example Black could

go wrong with 33...♞h6, when 34 ♖xh6! gxh6 35 ♖xh6 wins - Black loses his e-pawn or his g-pawn; if 35...♚g7 36 ♖f6. Yusupov, whose nickname is the Russian Wall, is not to be perturbed. He defends quietly.

34 ♖h7 ♖c6
35 ♖1h5

35 ... ♖c8

In his notes in *Informator 57*, Kamsky gives this move an exclamation-mark and says it is the only move. But what happens after 35...♖a6 instead? White must carry out his threat of 36 ♞g5 ♞xg5 37 ♖h8+ ♚f7 38 ♖xg5 g6! 39 ♖xe8 (39 ♖h7+ ♚f8 40 ♖xb7 ♝f7! followed by ...♖xa3. The rook on g5 is immured, so Black draws easily.) 39...♚xe8 40 ♖xg6 *(D)*

40...♚f7 41 ♖f6+ ♚e7 (41...♚g7!?) 42 g5 ♖xa3 43 g6 ♖a1 44 ♖f7+ ♚e8 45 ♖xb7 ♖g1 46 g7 a5 47 ♖a7 a4 48 ♚e3 a3 49 ♚f4 a2 50 ♖xa2 ♖xg7 51 ♖a8+ ♚f7 52 ♖a7+ ♚f8 53 ♖xg7 ♚xg7 54 ♚g5 and White wins - by one

tempo. If his king were still on f4, Black could play 54...♚g6 drawing. Can Black gain a tempo and draw?

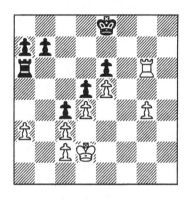

(analysis diagram)

Yes! At move 40 (see diagram above) he can play 40...♚e7! not giving White the opportunity to play 41 ♖f6 with check. Now 41 ♖f6 ♖xa3 42 g5 ♖a1 43 g6 ♖g1 44 ♖f7+ ♚e8 draws, as does 41 ♖g7+ ♚f8 42 ♖xb7 ♖xa3.

So Black could have forced a draw with 35...♖a6!. However, it was not easy to see this during the game - indeed, Kamsky did not see it in his post-game analysis. I suspect Yusupov did not think he was in any danger if he defended passively; and to a certain extent, he was right. However, this lack of vigilance eventually proves his undoing.

36 ♚e3 a5

It was still possible to play 36...♖c6. However, White's king is one square up the board if White goes in for the variation with 37 ♘xg5, etc., as above. This could prove crucial. Yusupov prefers to strengthen the blockade on the queenside, and evacuate a pawn from the second rank. This proves useful in a variation such as 37 ♘xg5 ♘xg5 38 ♖h8+ ♔f7 39 ♖xg5 g6 40 ♖h7+ ♔g8 41 ♖xb7 ♗f7 followed by ...♔g7, as given by Kamsky. White's g5 rook is in the now familiar trap. The drawback to 36...a5 is that Black permanently loses the option of ...♖a6 attacking the a-pawn.

37   ♖h1   a4

Not 37...♗a4 38 ♘xg5! ♗xc2 39 ♖h7-h2.

38   ♖7h2   b5

Now Black has fixed the queenside. White's rooks or king cannot hope to break through there. However, more and more Black pawns are ending up on white squares. This restricts the bishop on e8. So it is time for White to consider playing ♖xg5! to force a favourable material balance: a rook and good knight against a rook and bad bishop.

39   ♖f2

White probes a little while longer...

39	...	♖c7
40	♖h5	♖e7
41	♖f1	♖b7
42	♔f2	♖b6?!

... and Black carelessly plays his rook to an inferior square. Obviously, his sense of danger has been dulled by White's endless manoeuvres. 42...♖c7 was

better, or indeed anywhere else on the second rank. The reason why becomes apparent as the game progresses.

43   ♔g3   ♖a6?!

The rook could still return to the second rank, and no serious damage would be done.

44   ♖xg5!   ♘xg5
45   ♘xg5   ♗g6

If the rook were on the second rank, Black could play 45...♖e7 here and there would be little to fear. His rook could defend the e-pawn and be in contact with the kingside. On a6, on the other hand, although the rook defends the e-pawn, it is out of touch with the kingside. This gives White the chance of a breakthrough.

46	♖f2	♖b6
47	♔h4	♖a6
48	♘h3	

48   ...   ♗e4?

Black's first serious mistake. He had two drawing methods:

a) 48...♖a7 49 ♘f4 ♖f7 50 ♔g3 ♖xf4!! 51 ♔xf4 ♗e8 and I can't see how White breaks through.

b) 48...♖a7 49 ♘f4 ♗f7 50 g5 planning, after 50...♖e7, either 51 g6, 52 ♔g5, 53 ♖h2, 54 ♖h7, 55 ♘h5 and then a spectacular breakthrough with 56 ♘f6+!?, or 51 g6, 52 ♔h5, 53 ♘h3, 54 ♘g5, 55 ♘h7, hoping for a mate on f8, or if Black prevents it with ...♖e8, a breakthrough on the seventh rank with ♖f7.

The common denominator in these plans is 51 g6, so Black must play the ugly move 50...g6! himself. Now Black's bishop is wretched, but it is still doing good defensive work, overprotecting e6 and g6 and ready to defend the b-pawn with ...♗e8 if necessary. Black's blockade holds, e.g. 51 ♘g2 ♔g7 52 ♘e3 ♖e8 53 ♘g4 ♖e7 and now 54 ♘h6 ♗e8 55 ♖f6 ♗d7 etc., or 54 ♘f6 ♖c7 55 ♔g4 ♖c8 56 ♖h2 ♖h8! (or 56...♗g8) stopping White's plan of ♖h7+.

White's problem after 50...g6! is that there are no breakthrough squares for his king - the position is simply too blocked. If you remove White's e5 pawn then White, despite being a pawn down, can win by ♔f4 and ♔e5, penetrating with his king.

49 ♔h5!

The black bishop suddenly finds it cannot get back to g6 to cover f7. What's more, the bishop is a target on e4. The blockade begins to crumble.

49 ... ♖a7

If 49...♖b6 then 50 ♘g5 followed by 51 ♖f7 infiltrating.

50 ♘g5 ♖e7

If 50...♗h7 51 ♘xe6 wins.

51 ♘xe4 dxe4
52 ♔g6

White now has a winning endgame. The finish is instructive:

52 ... e3!

The path of maximum resistance. Black activates his rook.

53 ♖e2 ♖f7
54 ♖xe3 ♖f2
55 ♖e1!

Finding the breakthrough plan.

55 ... ♖xc2
56 ♖b1 ♖xc3
57 ♖xb5

Material is now even, but White's king dominates his counterpart.

57 ... ♔f8
58 ♖b4 ♖xa3
59 ♖xc4 ♖a1
60 g5 a3
61 ♖a4 a2
62 ♖a7 ♔e8

No better is 62...♖d1 63 ♖xa2 ♖xd4 64 ♖a8+ ♔e7 65 ♔xg7 and the g-pawn will run through.

63 ♔xg7 ♔d8
64 g6 ♔e8
65 ♖a6 ♔e7
66 ♖a8 ♔d7
67 ♔g8 ♔e7
68 ♖a7+ ♔e8
69 g7 ♖h1

Or else White plays 70 ♔h7 ♖h1+ 71 ♔g6 ♖g1+ 72 ♔f6 and ♔xe6.

70 ♖xa2

Now if all the centre pawns - on d4, e5 and e6 - are removed,

White has a standard book win with 71 ♖e2+ ♔d7 72 ♖e4! followed by bringing out the king and sheltering it from checks with the rook (the so-called Lucena position). So White has to get rid of the centre pawns.

70...♔e7 71 ♖a7+ ♔e8 72 ♖a5 ♔e7 73 d5 exd5 74 ♖xd5 ♖h2 75 ♖c5 ♖h1 76 ♖a7+ ♔e8 77 e6 ♖h2 78 ♖f7! ♖h1 79 e7! ♖h2 80 ♖f8+ ♔e7 81 ♖f3 ♔e8 82 ♖e3+ ♔d7 83 ♖e4 1-0

White is ready to play 84 ♔f7 ♖f2+ 85 ♔g6 ♖g2+ 86 ♔f6 ♖f2+ 87 ♔g5 ♖g2+ 88 ♖g4.

A gritty display by Kamsky. Top-class chess is not for the fainthearted!

6   The Indian Bishop

The key feature of many modern opening systems (for example, the King's Indian, Grünfeld, and Sicilian Dragon) is the fianchetto of Black's king's bishop on g7. From g7 the bishop exerts pressure on White's centre, and (assuming Black has castled kingside) also has an important defensive function. Hence Black's strategy usually revolves around this piece. We shall look at some examples where, at slight material cost, Black succeeded in activating his 'Indian' bishop.

Adams-Khalifman
Las Palmas 1993

1 e4 c5 2 ♘f3 d6 3 d4 cxd4 4 ♘xd4 ♘f6 5 ♘c3 g6 6 ♗e2 ♗g7 7 0-0 0-0 8 ♗e3 ♘c6 9 ♔h1 d5!
White has played an innocuous system against the Dragon and Black has thoughts of taking the initiative, exploiting the power of his king's bishop. For example, if 10 exd5 ♘xd5 11 ♘xc6 bxc6 12 ♘xd5 cxd5 and the a1-h8 diagonal is swept clear (if 13 ♗d4 e5).

10	♘xc6	bxc6
11	e5	

White, for his part, wants the black bishop kept under lock and key. He plans to follow up with 12 f4 (say after 11...♘e8) when Black can only activate his bishop with a subsequent ...f7-f6, which will leave him with a compromised pawn structure after exf6 ♗xf6.

| 11 | ... | ♘e4! |

This fine move decides the battle for the bishop's future in Black's favour. If White plays 12 f4 then 12...♘xc3 shatters his queenside pawn structure, so he must exchange knights. This, however, means that the e-pawn becomes very hard to defend, since if f2-f4, Black captures *en passant*.

12	♘xe4	dxe4
13	♕xd8	♖xd8
14	♖fd1	♗e6

14...♖xd1+ 15 ♖xd1 ♗xe5 16 ♖d8+ ♔g7 would be very dangerous for Black. For instance, White could play 17 ♗a6 ♗b7 18 ♖xa8 ♗xa8 19 ♗xa7 when the a-pawn would be difficult to stop.

15   &d4

White is reduced to artificial methods to defend the e-pawn. The aggressive 15 &xd8+ &xd8 16 &xa7 looks suspicious after 16...&xe5 (and 17...&xb2) or 16...&d2.

15   ...   f5!

16   a4?

White thinks he has solved the problem of Black's g7 bishop and so plays to gain space on the queenside. His ideas include advancing the a-pawn to a6 and then playing the rook to a5 and c5 in order to intensify the pressure on Black's split queenside pawns. However, he had overlooked Black's plan. As Khalifman points out, he should play 16 exf6 &xf6 17 &xf6 exf6 with equality.

16   ...   &f7

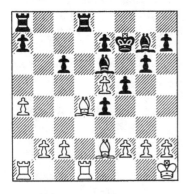

17   a5?

17 c3! was better, bolstering the bishop on d4. Then 17...&b3 18 &e1 (not 18 &d2 c5) and if 18...&e6? 19 &a3! &db8 (19...&d5 20 c4) 20 &xb3!, or

18...&d5 19 &a3 &c2? 20 &c4. Black's best line is probably 18...c5 19 e6+!? &xe6 20 &xc5 &d2 21 &a3 &b3 with pressure.

17   ...   &xd4!

Our positional sacrifice. The Indian bishop will finally come to life.

18   &xd4   &b8!

Adams may have allowed the sacrifice because he missed or underestimated the strength of this move. After 18...&xe5? 19 &b4 White would have fair chances: his queenside pawn structure remains intact and his rook is well placed. On the other hand, after 18...&b8, not only is White's rook denied activity on the b-file, but even worse, he cannot prevent Black playing ...&xb2, winning a pawn and fragmenting the remaining queenside pawns. However, as will be seen, all is not yet lost for White.

17...&xd4 is a typical positional or long-term sacrifice, yet it depends for its validity on the

'tactical' move 18...♖b8. If White's rook on a1 were on any other first-rank square - say e1 - then 18...♖b8 could be answered by the simple 19 b3. Only in the game position with the rook on a1 is 19 b3 impossible because 19...♗xe5 wins the exchange by skewering the two rooks.

So was Khalifman lucky? Is it a sheer fluke that the rook was on a1 and not f1 or c1? The fact is that the dynamics of the struggle never gave White the tempo he needed to play ♖f1 or ♖c1. There was always something else that he was required to do. Tartakower defined chess as 'the tragedy of one tempo', while Bronstein talked of 'the most powerful weapon in chess - the next move!' The time element in chess - the 'rhythm' of the game, as it were - is so important that it should not be surprising that the most positional of sacrifices should stand or fall on whose turn to move it is.

19 f4?

Now in order to win the e-pawn, Black must exchange off his own strong e4 pawn, and allow the white bishop some activity. If 19 ♗c4 ♗xe5 20 ♗xe6+ ♔xe6 21 ♖c4 ♔d5 is hopeless, or 19 ♖b1 ♗xe5 20 ♖a4 ♖xb2 (20...♖d8!?) and Black has a clear advantage. These variations are given by Khalifman in *Informator 58*.

One wonders if Khalifman is being somewhat optimistic about

Black's chances after 20 ♖a4 in the second variation. The exchange of Black's remaining rook is inevitable after both 20...♖xb2 or 20...♖d8!? 21 ♖d1. It is a well-known principle that when you are the exchange up in an endgame you should try to force off the opponent's remaining rook, so that he has no piece left which can act at long range across the board. After 20...♖xb2 21 ♖xb2 ♗xb2 22 ♔g1, White has good survival chances. But note that the alternative 22 ♖b4 ♗c3 23 ♖b7 ♗xa5 24 ♖xa7 is not satisfactory for White. As has just been remarked, the rook acts at greater range. Therefore it helps Black to exchange off the pawns at the periphery of the board, since he is less likely to be overstretched. 22 ♗c4 ♗d5! is also not good.

Black's winning hope is his impressive mass of pawns in the centre, but its hard to believe that White should lose if he defends well. White can also generate counterplay with 22 a6, 23 ♖b4 and 24 ♖b7. So the assessment 'slight advantage to Black' seems more appropriate. Of course, this does not devalue the sacrifice, which was undoubtedly correct. It does mean, however, that a question mark must be added to the move 19 f4.

19 ... exf3
20 ♗xf3 ♗xe5
21 ♖d3
Or 21 ♖d2 ♖xb2 22 ♗xc6 ♗c3

winning the c-pawn, e.g. 23 ♖e2 ♗c4 24 ♖f2 ♗d4 25 ♖f4 e5.

| **21** | **...** | **♖xb2** |

The difference between the game continuation and the variations examined at move 19 is that Black does not have to allow the exchange of his rook in capturing this pawn. The rook is dominant on the seventh rank, so the difference decides whether Black has a small advantage or a decisive one.

22	♖e1	♗d6
23	♗xc6	♖xc2
24	♗d5	♗xd5
25	♖xd5	♖a2!

This wins the a-pawn.

26	g3	♗b4
27	♖b1	♖xa5
28	♖d7	

28 ♖xa5 ♗xa5 is equally hopeless. The outside a-pawn would be unstoppable.

28...♔e6 29 ♖d8 ♗d6 30 ♖h8 h5 31 ♖f8 ♖e5 32 ♖b2 a5 33 ♖a2 ♗b4 34 ♔g2 ♔d5 35 ♖c2 a4 36 ♖g8 ♖e6 37 ♖d8+ ♗d6 38 ♖d2+ ♔c6 39 ♖a8 a3 40 ♔f3 ♖e4 41 ♖g8 ♖b4!

| 42 | ♖c8+ | |

There was not time to capture the g-pawn. Khalifman gives 42 ♖xg6 ♖b3+ 43 ♔e2 ♖b2 44 ♖g8 ♗b4!.

42	...	♔b5
43	♖d5+	♔b6
44	♖a8	

The white rooks have fought valiantly to prevent Black's plan of bringing his king to b3 in order

to shepherd home the passed pawn. However, in keeping the king out, they have allowed a blow from rook and bishop:

44	...	♖b3+
45	♔e2	♖b2+
46	♖d2	

If 46 ♔d3 ♖xh2 followed by...♖g2, and Black will shortly have five passed pawns.

| 46 | ... | ♗b4 |
| | **0-1** | |

The pawn will queen.

Santo-Roman-M.Gurevich
Clichy 1993

---

1 e4 d6 2 d4 ♘f6 3 ♘c3 g6 4 ♗g5 c6 5 ♕d2 ♗g7 6 ♘f3 0-0 7 h3 ♘bd7

Here rather than develop (8 ♗e2) or restrain Black on the queenside (8 a4), White tried to exploit Black's last move with

8 e5!?

since normally Black plays 7...b5 and answers 8 e5 with the counter-attacking 8...b4!.

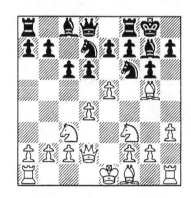

After 8...♘e8 9 0-0-0 White has the makings of a big attack with h4-h5. The white e5 pawn is immune after 9...dxe5 10 dxe5 because of the pin on the d-file, and Black's queen cannot easily move from d8 without allowing ♗xe7. Furthermore, 9...f6 cannot be played without weakening the central pawn structure. And finally 9...b5 10 h4 b4 11 ♘e4 (attacking d6) 11...d5 12 ♘g3 ♕a5 13 ♔b1 leaves the bishop on g7 shut out of the game and White ready to play 14 h5. If 13...h5?, then 14 e6! fxe6 15 ♗d3 ♔h7 16 ♘xh5. Evidently, Gurevich did not like the look of these variations and found a dynamic alternative involving an exchange sacrifice:

8 ... dxe5!
9 dxe5 ♘d5!
10 ♘xd5 cxd5
11 ♗h6

As Gurevich points out, 11 ♕xd5? ♘xe5 12 ♕xd8 ♘xf3+ 13 gxf3 ♖xd8 is bad for White. His initiative is gone and he is left with weak kingside pawns. Instead, Santo-Roman defends his e-pawn by indirect means. He hopes to start a strong attack after 11...e6 12 h4, etc. But now we see the point of Black's play:

11 ... ♘xe5!
Crossing White's plans.
12 ♘xe5 ♗xe5
13 ♗xf8 ♔xf8 (D)

Black has seized the initiative. His bishop on e5 is tremendously strong and there is an immediate threat of ...♗xb2. White cannot play 14 0-0-0 without facing a huge attack after 14...♕b6 15 c3 ♗e6 and ...♖c8 (Gurevich). Sacrificial ideas against c3 would flow naturally from such a position. Also, ...d5-d4 is a strong threat. In general, it is very double-edged to castle queenside into the line of fire of a black bishop on the a1-h8 diagonal; unless of course you have strong defences along this diagonal and have a rapid kingside attack as compensation. In the present example, White has neither strong defences nor a kingside attack. Therefore, 14 0-0-0 would be particularly foolhardy, and White has to prepare kingside castling.

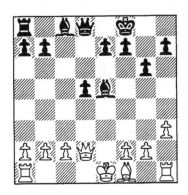

14 c3 ♕c7!
Gurevich's best move of the game. His plan is to eventually play ...d5-d4 increasing the scope of his e5 bishop. The best square for the bishop on c8 is therefore c6 where it will control an open diagonal after the d-pawn advances. It will also aim at the g2

square which could prove unpleasant for White's king. After 14...♕c7! the d-pawn is immune for tactical reasons: 15 ♕xd5? ♗xc3+!, etc.

| 15 | ♗e2 | ♗d7 |
| 16 | 0-0 | ♗c6 |

Now that White has completed his development, he has to form a plan. The reader will be familiar with the dictum that rooks need open lines. Therefore, White must try to puncture a hole somewhere in Black's solid wall of pawns. But how? If he prepares and carries out the advance c4, then Black can reply ...d5-d4 with a powerful passed pawn, and no open lines anyway. Or if he doubles rook on the e-file, Black simply plays ...e7-e6 and there is no breakthrough. So Santo-Roman tries using his f-pawn, but this proves bad as well.

Since all active plans fail, White should probably wait and see what Black comes up with. For example, if Black decides on an eventual ...e7-e5 and ...d5-d4 to create a passed pawn in the centre and activate the c6 bishop, then after White's cxd4 and the recapture ...exd4, both the e- and c-files will be open, and this will give White counterplay. Black's position at present is defensively very strong, but if he wants to win he has to allow some chinks to appear in his armour. But it is psychologically difficult to do nothing and, as we saw in the chapter on depriving the oppo-

nent of a plan, not usually a very rewarding strategy.

| 17 | f4?! | ♗f6 |
| 18 | ♖ad1 | |

After 18 f5 g5! the f-file remains closed and White is left very weak on the b8-h2 diagonal. He would have to watch out for a sudden ...♕g3 and ...♗e5 with a winning attack. So all 17 f4 has done is weaken White's kingside.

18	...	♔g7
19	♗f3	e6
20	g3	

Besides further weakening the kingside, this allows a tactical blow which leads to a fragmented queenside. Gurevich recommends 20 a3 ♗a4 21 ♖de1 ♖d8 22 ♔h1. Black has the initiative but he must still find a way to break through without allowing counterplay.

20	...	♕a5!
21	a3	♗a4!
22	♖c1	d4

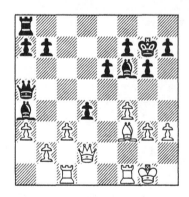

The point of Black's play. White's pawns are broken up since 23 ♗xb7? dxc3 24 bxc3

♕b6+ wins a piece, or 23 b4 dxc3 24 ♖xc3 ♕b6+ 25 ♖c5 ♖d8 followed by ...♗d4+.

23	♔h2	dxc3
24	bxc3	♖d8
25	♕b2	b6
26	♕b4	

This allows the black rook to penetrate. But 26 ♖f2 ♖d3 intending ...♗xc3 was very unpleasant. Note the enormous power of the bishop on f6.

| 26 | ... | ♖d2+ |
| 27 | ♔h1 | ♕a6! |

Black does not want to exchange queens since the whole king is vulnerable.

28 c4

White has no remaining constructive ideas. Perhaps he should have played the desperate 28 g4 hoping to dislodge the black bishop with 29 g5.

28 ... ♖d3!

A nasty move to meet in time pressure. White probably expected 28...♖b2 when 29 ♕d6, with the idea of creating a passed pawn with c4-c5, gives White counterplay. 28...♖d3! denies the queen the d6 square and unexpectedly wins the a-pawn.

29 ♔h2

Ruling out any ideas of...♖xf3 and ...♗c6 pinning the rook.

29 ... ♗e8!

And suddenly the white a-pawn is lost. A remarkable retreat by the bishop. Gurevich is accurate to the end, since 29...♗d7, a more plausible retreat, allows 30 ♖cd1.

30 c5?

A time pressure blunder but 30 a4 ♕xa4 was bad anyway. The black a7 pawn would prove very strong in combination with the dominant bishop on f6.

30 ... bxc5

Gurevich's only slip in a finely played game. 30...♖xf3! wins immediately.

31 ♖xc5

31 ♕xc5 avoids an immediate finish, but 31...♖xa3 leaves Black in total control: Black's kingside is rock solid and he can prepare the advance of the a-pawn. White would be hindered in his attempt to stop the passed pawn by the need to protect his precariously placed king. Now however it is all over.

31 ... ♖xf3!

0-1

32 ♖xf3 ♕e2+ wins the rook.

Novik-Gallagher
Oberwart 1993

1 ♘f3 ♘f6 2 c4 g6 3 d4 ♗g7 4 ♘c3 0-0 5 e4 d6 6 ♗e2 e5 7 d5 a5 8 h3 ♘a6 9 ♗g5 ♕e8 10 ♘d2 ♘d7 11 g4

A typical King's Indian battle is in full swing. Black's basic plan is to achieve the ...f7-f5 advance in order to dissolve White's e-pawn and liberate his g7 bishop with ...e5-e4. So he has played ...♕e8, breaking the pin, and then ...♘d7, clearing the way for the f-pawn. White of course is doing his best to obstruct this plan, or to make sure that it turns out disadvantageously for Black. So he began with ♗g5, pinning the black knight; then he retreated the knight to d2 in order to bolster the e4 square with f2-f3 after ...f7-f5; lastly he played 11 g4 preventing ...f7-f5 for tactical reasons: 11...f5? 12 gxf5 gxf5 13 ♗h5 and wins.

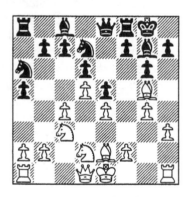

11   ...   ♘dc5

This clears the d7 square for the queen, so that in the ...f7-f5 variation above, ♗h5 can be answered by ...♕d7.

12   ♖g1

Another tactical variation to dissuade ...f7-f5: 12...f5 13 gxf5 gxf5 14 ♗h6 ♖f7 15 ♗h5 and wins. So Black moves his king out of the potential pin.

12   ...   ♔h8!

White has now come to the end of his tricks to 'prevent' ...f7-f5. Novik and Nesis in *Informator 58* now give the laconic '13 ♗e3 f5 14 f3=', but this would undoubtedly represent a minor victory for

Black, since White's strategy would have failed, i.e. he would have lost the initiative. Novik is not prepared to give Black easy equality after only 12 moves and continues to play for advantage: a psychologically understandable, if incorrect, decision.

13   ♘f1?!

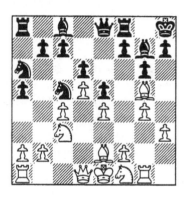

13   ...   c6

As Novik and Nesis point out, there was no reason for Black to avoid the natural 13...f5, e.g. 14 gxf5 gxf5 15 exf5 ♗xf5. Black has an active position and is ready to play ...e5-e4, opening up the diagonal for his g7 bishop and at the same time introducing the idea of ...♘d3+. The annotators also point out the variation 15 ♗h5 (instead of 15 exf5) 15...♕d7 16 ♘g3 f4 17 ♘f5 (D) 17...♘xe4! with a clear advantage to Black. Novik may have missed 17...♘xe4 when he played 13 ♘f1. Otherwise, the plan of ♘f1-g3-f5 would have been a very good one: the knight would be excellently placed, the g7 bishops diagonal blocked and the g-file an avenue of attack against Black's king.

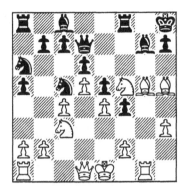

(analysis diagram)

And likewise, Gallagher may have avoided 13...f5 because he did not see the tactic 17...♘xe4 which saves him from unpleasant pressure (and gives him a big advantage). If this interpretation of events is correct, then it demonstrates how important it is to be alert to the subtleties of the game. Both players made a positional error because they missed a tactical point. Of course, if you have very fine positional judgement, or have a strong sense of justice, you could play 13...f5! without thinking and stumble 'by accident' on 17...♘xe4. The problem is that chess is not always a just game - moves which are 'natural' or 'logical' or 'interesting' often founder 'undeservedly' on an obscure tactical point. There is not always a move like 17...♘xe4 to save the innocent. And you

would need an exceptional feel for chess to know intuitively whether or not a move can be tactically refuted four moves down the line.

14 ♘g3

Now White assumes the initiative again. If 14...f5, White could play 15 gxf5 gxf5 16 ♘h5! (16 ♗h5!?) eliminating the g7 bishop with a good game.

14	...	cxd5
15	cxd5	♗d7
16	h4	

Planning to ram the h-pawn down the throat of the g7 bishop. Black barricades his kingside and looks for counterplay on the queenside:

16	...	b5
17	♕d2	b4
18	♘d1	f6
19	♗e3	♕e7
20	h5	gxh5
21	f3!	

21 ♘xh5 allows 21...♘xe4. Or if 21 gxh5 f5! and Black has achieved his thematic advance. White therefore prefers to sacrifice a pawn in order to keep a grip on the f5 square. If he can prevent Black playing ...f7-f5, then the bishop on g7 - the key black piece - will either remain shut out of the game, or vulnerable to exchange by ♘h5xg7, when the dark squares in Black's kingside will be left weak. Grandmaster Gallagher is fully aware of the danger facing him and, realising that passive play is useless, returns the pawn to free

his bishop.

21	...	hxg4
22	fxg4	f5!

Playing the impossible move. Now 23 ♘xf5 ♗xf5 24 exf5 e4 and the bishop sees daylight; if 25 ♗d4 ♘d3+! 26 ♗xd3 ♗xd4. 23 exf5 e4! is similar. Therefore, White has no choice:

23	gxf5	♗f6
24	♘f2	♖ac8?

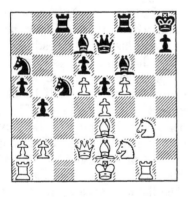

Curiously, Nesis and Novik do not criticise this move, although it amounts to a loss of tempo, but they do mention 24...♗h4! which is undoubtedly stronger: the

bishop completes its journey to activity. After 25 0-0-0 ♖g8 26 ♘gh1! the knight which terrorised Black with ideas of ♘f5 ends up on a ridiculous square. The expression Black has dynamic counterplay seems appropriate here.

25	♗xa6?!

With this exchange White takes off the pressure of e4 before playing ♘h5 eliminating the black f6 bishop. The immediate 25 ♘h5 allows a combination 25...♗h4 26 ♗xa6 ♘xe4 27 ♕e2 ♘xf2 28 ♗xf2 ♗xf2+ 29 ♕xf2 ♖xf5 (Nesis and Novik). The piece sacrifice has broken open the centre and we are suddenly reminded that White also has a king. However, the assessment clear advantage to Black in *Informator* seems incorrect, since there is no clear continuation for Black after 30 ♕h2. The rook on c8 is attacked and the threat of ♖g7 may be dangerous. Hence the sacrifice is dubious. Therefore, White should play 25 ♘h5 immediately when after 25...♖g8 26 ♖xg8+ ♖xg8 27 0-0-0 we reach a position similar to the game, but with the bishop still on e2 and the knight on a6. The difference favours White since the offside knight is a much worse piece than the bishop.

25	...	♘xa6
26	♘h5	♖g8

26...♗h4 27 ♗h6 is bad for Black, but now he loses by exchange his prize dark-squared bishop.

27	🜚xg8+	🜚xg8
28	0-0-0	

28   ...   ♘c5

Black cannot keep the bishop: 28...♗h4 29 ♕e2! ♘c5 30 ♕f3 ♗e8 31 🜚h1 ♗xf2 32 ♗xf2 ♕g5+ 33 ♗e3 ♗xh5 34 ♗xg5 ♗xf3 35 ♗f6+ 🜚g7 36 🜚g1 wins, or at move 31, 31...♗xh5 32 ♕xh5 ♗xf2 33 ♗xc5! ♗xc5 34 f6 ♕c7 35 f7 🜚g1+ 36 🜚d2 ♗e3+ 37 🜚d3 and mate on h7. These pretty variations are given by Nesis and Novik.

29	♘xf6	♕xf6
30	♗xc5	dxc5
31	♘d3	

White has eliminated the Indian bishop and has a much superior pawn structure. He now plans to answer 31...c4 with 32 ♘c5 followed by d6, when the passed pawn is very powerful.

31	...	♗b5
32	🜚b1	

The c-pawn is of course taboo.

32	...	c4
33	♘c5	🜚c8

34   ♘e6

In time pressure, White missed the strength of 34 d6! 🜚xc5 35 d7 ♗xd7 (35...♕d8 36 ♕d6 🜚c7 37 ♕xc7! wins, or 36...♕xd7 37 ♕f8 mate, or 36...🜚c6 37 ♕xe5+ 🜚g8 38 🜚g1+ wins) 36 ♕xd7 and Black's king is defenceless, e.g. 36...♕f8 37 🜚h1 ♕g8 38 ♕e7 🜚c8 39 ♕xe5+ ♕g7 40 f6 and wins (Nesis and Novik). In the absence of the g7 bishop, Black's king is often vulnerable.

34	...	c3!
35	♕c2	a4

36   🜚h1?

Panic in time pressure. White's problem is that he has wrested a definite positional advantage from the tactical mêlée, but now he can't find a way to kill off the dynamism in the position and quietly enjoy this advantage. The threat of 36...b3 37 axb3 axb3 38 ♕xb3 c2+ should be met by 36 bxc3! ♖xc3 37 ♕b2 ♗d3+ 38 ♔a1 when 38...♕e7 (defending b4) 39 ♕h2 ♕f6 40 ♖h1 wins (Nesis and Novik). But it is difficult to be rational in time trouble.

| 36 | ... | b3! |
| 37 | axb3 | |

37 ♕h2 ♗d3+ 38 ♔a1 cxb2+ 39 ♕xb2 ♖c2 and 40...b2+ wins.

37	...	axb3
38	♕xb3	♗d3+
39	♔c1	♕e7!

But not 39...♗xe4 40 ♕b7! threatening mate by both 41 ♕xh7 and 41 ♕xc8+. Now, with his flag about to fall, White has to find a move that doesn't lose. According to Nesis and Novik, there is only one move: 40 ♕b6! to prevent the threatened 40...♕a7 and introduce the idea of 41 d6. Of course, it is no surprise that White does not find this move.

| 40 | bxc3? | ♗xe4 |
| 41 | ♖e1 | |

The only way to prevent 41...♕a7 which would threaten both 42...♕e3+ and 42...♕a1+. But now the queen infiltrates through a different route:

| 41 | ... | ♕h4! |
| 42 | ♖d1 | ♕g3 |

| 43 | ♘c7 | |

A desperate attempt to block the c-file. White's king faces the all-out attack of Black's pieces, and there is hardly any pawn cover. It is no wonder his position soon collapses.

43...♕e3+ 44 ♔b2 ♖g8! 45 ♘b5 ♕e2+ 46 ♔a3 ♗c2 47 ♖e1 ♖a8+ 48 ♔b2 ♕xe1 49 ♔xc2 ♕e2+ 50 ♔b1 ♖g8! 0-1

The change of front is decisive.

Arencibia-Akopian
Biel 1993

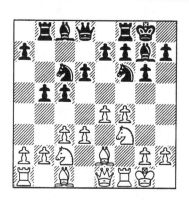

Black began the process of undermining White's centre with

| 10 | ... | b4! |

Now White should try 11 c4 when Black undoubtedly has the better of it since White is weak on the diagonal a1-h8 and the d4 square in particular is a 'hole'. However, White's centre structure would remain intact and the closed nature of the position would minimise Black's advantage. In the game, White did not want to admit his strategy had gone awry and so he played a perfunctory developing move:

| 11 | ♗d2? | bxc3 |
| 12 | ♗xc3 | |

If 12 bxc3 c4! splits White's centre pawns. Perhaps Arencibia thought he had neutralised the Indian bishop, but he is in for a rude awakening:

| 12 | ... | d5! |
| 13 | e5 | |

White's centre now loses all cohesion, but as Akopian points out, 13 exd5 ♘xd5 14 ♗xg7 ♔xg7 is clearly to Black's advantage. Both b2 and f4 are attacked, and if 15 ♕c1 then 15...♕b6 introduces ideas of ...♕xb2 or ...c5-c4+ and ...♘g4.

| 13 | ... | ♘h5! |

Already Akopian is planning a sacrifice to demolish White's overstretched centre.

| 14 | ♕c1 | f6! |
| 15 | d4? | |

Still refusing to accept how badly he stands. He should try 15 exf6 ♗xf6 16 ♗xf6 ♖xf6 17 g3, though 17...♗h3 or 17...♕b6 is still clearly good for Black. The game continuation is hopeless.

| 15 | ... | ♘xf4! |

Now White's whole centre disappears with remarkable rapidity.

16	♕xf4	fxe5
17	♕h4	exd4
18	♗d2	e5!

Black does not allow the exchange of his treasured dark-squared bishop: 18...♖xb2 19 ♗h6 followed by 20 ♘g5 and

White has attacking chances against Black's king (Akopian).

| 19 | ♗g5 | ♕c7 |
| 20 | ♘d2 | ♗f5 |

Black's pieces combine well with his massive pawn centre. There is no rush to advance the pawns since White has no counterplay or means to fortify his position.

| 21 | ♘e1 | e4 |
| 22 | ♗f4 | ♗e5 |

Now Black allows the exchange of his dark-squared bishop since White's knights have been driven far away from the black king's defensive perimeter.

| 23 | ♗xe5 | ♕xe5 |

An Indian queen to replace the Indian bishop.

24	♖b1	d3
25	♗g4	♕d4+
	0-1	

26 ♔h1 e3 wins the bishop on g4 to start with.

Black however does not always have it his own way. If White succeeds in keeping the Indian bishop immured then he will have an excellent game.

Epishin-Gheorghiu
Geneva 1993

(see following diagram)

| 13 | a5! | |

White has a space advantage. His natural plan is to prepare the pawn advance b2-b4 which begins the process of 'peeling' Black's centre. However, if White carelessly plays 13 ♖b1? then Black can answer 13...a5! which completely blocks the queenside and frustrates White's plan. Hence the move 13 a5, which also has another useful point that becomes clear on the next move.

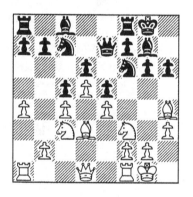

13   ...   ♕e8

Black's plan is consistent with the theme of this chapter: he prepares the advance ...f7-f5 in order to attack White's centre and perhaps eventually liberate the entombed bishop on g7. The game will be decided by how successfully Black is able to implement his strategy.

14   ♗c2!

White has seen through Black's intentions. If Black now plays 14...♘h7 (or 14...♘h5), aiming for the ...f7-f5 advance, then 15 ♗a4! forces him to agree (after 15...♗d7) to the positionally unfavourable exchange of his

'good' bishop for White's 'bad' bishop. This would mean that Black would be left with his miserable bishop on g7, which is blocked in by its own pawns, while White's bishop on h4 could be re-routed to active play after an eventual ♘d2, f3 and ♗f2. Play could continue 14...♘h7 15 ♗a4 ♗d7 16 ♗xd7 ♕xd7 17 ♕a4! ♕xa4 18 ♘xa4 (threatening 19 ♗e7) 18...♗f6 19 b4!

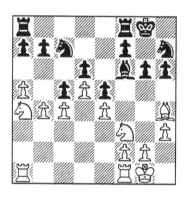

(analysis diagram)

Now 19...cxb4 20 c5 ♗xh4 21 ♘xh4 is clearly to White's advantage: he will soon win the pawn back and remain with a much better pawn structure after 21...dxc5 22 ♘xc5 followed by ♖ab1, etc. The protected passed pawn on d5 would be very strong. No better for Black is 19...♗xh4 20 bxc5! ♗f6 (20...♗e7 21 cxd6 ♗xd6 22 c5 and 23 d6 regains the piece with a winning position) 21 cxd6 ♘a6 22 c5 and the passed pawns are worth more than the piece, e.g. 22...♖fc8 23 ♖fc1 followed by 24 ♖ab1 or 24 c6.

In the game, Black avoided the bishop exchange but there were other problems to face:

14	...	♘d7
15	g4!	

If the knight were on h7, Black could now play 15...f5, achieving the freeing ...f7-f5 advance and breaking up White's kingside. But because the knight is on d7, obstructing the action of the bishop on c8, White can simply answer 15...f5 with 16 exf5 gxf5 17 ♗xf5 winning a pawn. Therefore, Black's natural plan is thwarted, at least for the moment. Epishin tries to achieve a vice-like grip on the f5 square, and so permanently prevent ...f7-f5.

15	...	♗f6
16	♗g3	

White does not allow Black to ease the congestion in his ranks by exchanging bishops.

16	...	♔g7
17	♕d2	♕e7
18	♔g2	♖h8

An admission that his plan of ...f7-f5 has been defeated. Black waits patiently to see how White can strengthen his position.

19	h4?!	

More accurate was in fact 19 ♘d1! immediately.

19	...	♕d8
20	♘d1	

White brings his knight to the excellent e3 square as the prelude to a direct attack on Black's centre and kingside. This strategy is now more promising than the preparation of the b4 advance, since Black's queenside is well fortified by three minor pieces and a rook.

20	...	b5?

Gheorghiu tires of his passive defence. He should play 20...♗e7!. Then 21 ♘e3 ♘f6 attacks g4, and now 22 ♘h2 ♘d7 23 ♘f3 (else the h-pawn drops) 23...♘f6 is a draw by repetition. Alternatively, White could sacrifice a piece: 22 ♘xe5 dxe5 23 ♗xe5 followed by the advancing of his centre pawns en masse. But White's preparations for this sacrifice are not as complete as they are in the game at move 28 when he plays a similar sacrifice. Black can continue to fish in troubled waters with 23...♔g8, e.g. 24 ♕c3 (better is 24 ♖ad1) 24...♘ce8, etc.

If White had played 19 ♘d1! instead of the premature 19 h4?!, Black would not have had this defensive option: the g-pawn would remain defended. Gheorghiu however misses his chance and chases some will-of-the wisp on the queenside.

21	axb6	♘xb6
22	♘e3	♘a6
23	♖h1	♘b4

A rather useless manoeuvre with the knight which chases the white bishop to a better square and does nothing to stop White's methodical kingside build-up. It would have been better to keep both knights on or near the kingside, where they would help defend against White's inevitable breakthrough.

| 24 | ♗d1 | ♗d7 |
| 25 | ♗e2 | a5 |

Black's 'attack' on the queenside continues. Unfortunately for him, there is nothing to attack. Now White feels ready to act.

| 26 | g5! | hxg5 |
| 27 | hxg5 | |

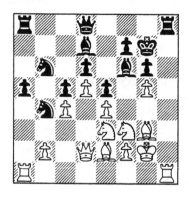

| 27 | ... | ♗e7 |

As Epishin points out, 27...♗xg5? 28 ♘xg5 ♕xg5 29 ♘f5+ ♔f6 (forced) 30 ♕xg5+ ♔xg5 31 ♘xd6 wins. But now comes a thematic sacrifice:

28	♘xe5!	dxe5
29	♗xe5+	f6
30	♗c3!	

White has destroyed Black's centre, acquired two passed pawns and gained strong attacking chances against Black's king. Epishin's marvellously restrained 30th move threatens 31 d6 when the bishop on e7 dare not move, or 31 gxf6+ ♗xf6 32 e5 powering through in the centre. The bishop on c3 is enormously strong.

| 30 | ... | ♘a4 |

Black's only hope is to eliminate the white bishop.

| 31 | ♖xa4! | |

But this hope is dashed. White does not flinch from a further exchange sacrifice, since he knows that his central juggernaut will sweep all before it.

31	...	♖xh1
32	♔xh1	♗xa4
33	♘g4	

Now f6 drops and Black's position collapses before the rampaging pawns.

33	...	♕h8+
34	♔g1	♔f8
35	gxf6	♗d6
36	e5	♗c7
37	♕e3!	♘a6
38	e6	♗d6
39	e7+!	1-0

39...♔e8 40 f7+ wins the queen, or 39...♔f7 40 ♕e6+ and mate next move. A fine game by Epishin.

7   The 'Karpovian' Exchange Sacrifice

Every strong player knows that you need a plan. It may be a grand strategy that lasts many moves, or a simple tactical manoeuvre, but it is important to be doing something to enhance your position. Otherwise, the opponent will have endless time to strengthen his game, and if his position gets better, then perforce your position will get worse.

Karpov's speciality is depriving his opponent of a plan. Petursson, the Icelandic grandmaster, has played both Kasparov and Karpov. He sums up their different styles as follows: 'When you play Kasparov, you know he wants to annihilate you; when you play Karpov, nothing special happens, but you lose.'

Here are some examples of nothing much happening followed by top-class opposition biting the dust:

Karpov-Gelfand
Linares 1993

Black's pawn structure is ragged, but his activity apparently outweighs his positional deficiencies. For example, if 20 ♗d3 ♖g8 intending ...f7-f5 (Karpov), and Black will have enormous pressure along the a8-h1 diagonal. In the game, Karpov found a way to kill off the dynamism in Black's position. He began with:

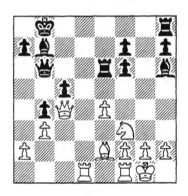

20   ♖d5!!
when Gelfand initially turned down the exchange offer. It is worth making a few observations about the position after the hypothetical 20...♗xd5 21 exd5 ♖e7 *(D)*.

Rooks thrive on open lines. The disappearance of Black's

bishop on b7 means that Black can no longer hope to strike a blow against g2 (after ...♖g8).

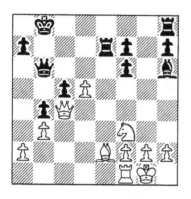

(analysis diagram)

Therefore, the only means of activity for Black's rooks is along the e-file. However, after 22 ♖d1 ♖he8 23 ♗d3, for example, all the breakthrough squares in White's position are guarded. Black's rooks are dressed up with nowhere to go.

So much for the rooks. It's also difficult to imagine how Black's bishop on h6 is ever going to take part in a co-ordinated action of the pieces. The *opposite-coloured bishops* greatly favour White. There are beautiful open diagonals for the white bishop. From d3, it can threaten ♗xh7, acquiring a passed pawn which will prove useful in an endgame, or after ♗f5 it could help to push the d-pawn to d7. Finally, if White chose to launch a direct attack on Black's king, the bishops control or potential control of

squares such as b5, a6, b7 and c6 would prove vulnerable.

So White's absolute control of the white squares and the lack of open lines negates Black's material advantage. And when we add White's strong passed pawn and Black's exposed king to the 'evidence', it is easy to conclude that White has all the chances. Gelfand knows that a position without a plan contains the seeds of defeat. Hence, he refuses the sacrifice.

20   ...   ♖he8
20...f5 21 ♘e5 looks dangerous.

21   ♗d3   ♖d8
Still hoping for some counter-play after 22 ♖xd8 ♕xd8 23 ♕c2 f5!.

22   ♖d1
Karpov keeps an iron grip on the position. Black isn't allowed a ghost of activity.

22   ...   ♖ed6
23   ♗e2   ♗xd5
Gelfand finally gives in. However, 23...♕c6 24 ♖xd6 ♖xd6 25 ♖xd6 ♕xd6 26 ♕xf7 was bad, as 26...♗xe4? fails to 27 ♕e8+; and 23...♖xd5 24 exd5 ♕d6 25 ♕c2! is also unpleasant as 25...♗xd5? 26 ♗c4 followed by ♕d3 leaves Black in a fatal pin, and meanwhile White is threatening 26 ♕xh7 or 26 ♗c4 solidifying d5.

Now Black at least has the exchange as consolation for his misery, but we are effectively in the situation referred to in the note to move 20.

24   exd5   ♛b7

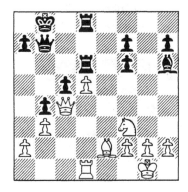

25   ♛h4!
Karpov's play consists of grand strategical strokes and an alertness to tactical nuances. If he were to lose the d5 pawn, then his whole positional build up would be proved wrong. But Karpov has calculated that he has just enough time to get in the vital ♗c4 move. He gives the following note in *Informator 57*:

a) 25...♖xd5? 26 ♖xd5 ♛xd5 27 ♛xh6 ♛d1+ 28 ♗f1!, or

b) 25...♗g5 26 ♛g3 ♛c7 27 ♗c4.

Hence the d5 pawn is inviolable. In his earlier calculations, Gelfand may have overlooked 28 ♗f1! in the first variation, or perhaps in the second variation he missed the quiet 26 ♛g3, gaining time for the vital ♗c4 by pinning the rook.

25   ...   ♗f8
26   ♗c4   ♖xd5
Black hastens to counter-sacrifice the exchange. After the alternative 26...h6 27 ♛e4 he

would be left without a constructive plan. It would be necessary to wait and see if White could strengthen his position. It's no wonder that this approach did not appeal to Gelfand. Nevertheless, patience is still a virtue and White would have to work hard to generate real winning chances. After 26...♖xd5 on the other hand, Black is left with weaknesses everywhere, and does not even have any material compensation.

27   ♗xd5   ♖xd5
28   ♖e1!
Of course he keeps the rooks on; this not only ensures the safety of White's king from back-rank checks, but also preserves threats against Black's exposed king.

28   ...   ♖d8
29   ♛xf6!
Karpov is determined not to give his opponent any counterplay whatsoever. The obvious 29 ♛xh7 allows 29...♛d5 with the idea of ...c5-c4!? followed by ...♗c5, when Black may get some attacking chances against f2 as well as White's queenside pawns. After 29 ♛xf6 ♛d5 Black does not threaten 30...c4 because of the simple 31 bxc4 since Black's rook on d8 needs defending.

29   ...   ♛c7
30   g3!   ♗d6
31   ♘g5
If Black had prevented this move with 30...h6 then 31 ♘e5

would have been equally strong. We now see the point of 30 g3!. If the white pawn were on g2, Black would have the trick 30...♗e7! avoiding the worst. Now however he must allow White to penetrate into his back rank with fatal consequences.

| 31 | ... | ♖d7 |
| 32 | ♖e8+ | |

Again Karpov prefers to keep control rather than allow Black counterplay after 32 ♘xh7 c4!.

32	...	♔b7
33	♘e4	♗e7
34	♕f5	

White sets his sight on the h-pawn. White can play 34 ♕xf7 safely, but there are many ways to win.

34	...	♕c6
35	♔g2	♖c7
36	♖h8	♕g6

It is too late for 36...c4 37 bxc4 ♕xc4 38 ♖xh7 ♕xa2(?) 39 ♕b5+ ♔c8 40 ♖h8+ ♗d8 41 ♘d6 mate.

37	♕d5+	♕c6
38	♕xc6+	♔xc6
39	♖xh7	♔d5

39...c4 40 bxc4 ♔d7 41 c5 is hopeless for Black.

40	♘d2	♗f6
41	♘c4	♔d4
42	♖h6	

The bad bishop plagues Black right until the end.

42	...	♖c6
43	g4	♖e6
44	h4	♔d5
45	g5	1-0

The passed pawn wins the day.

Lutz-Karpov
Dortmund 1993

White has just played 21 ♕h5 hoping for 21...♗xf4 22 gxf4 ♖xf4 23 e5! winning - Black must now defend or exchange his rook when 24 ♕xh7+ is decisive, and if 23...g6 24 ♗xg6!. Note how strong the white bishop becomes in this variation. Karpov found a way to frustrate White's plan:

| 21 | ... | ♖xf4! |
| 22 | gxf4 | ♗xf4+ |

It's vital that this is check. Otherwise, White would have time to play 23 e5.

| 23 | ♔b1 | ♕e5! |

Now, however, Black can ensure that White's bishop remains blocked in.

| 24 | ♕xe5 | |

After 24 ♕f3 ♖f8 25 ♖f2 g6! Black can play the manoeuvre ...♗h6-g7 aiming at b2. The black queen is much more powerfully placed than its white counterpart, so Lutz decides to exchange queens.

24 ... ♗xe5
25 h3

Its now time to sum up the consequences of Black's sacrifice. He has an absolutely safe game, without any weaknesses. The bishop on e5 is impregnable, and exerts influence across the whole board. Black's 2-1 majority of pawns on the kingside could later be converted into a passed pawn. There is no harmony among White's pieces and pawns. The pawns on c4 and e4, besides being vulnerable to attack, shut the bishop on d3 out of the game. White's rooks have few active opportunities. Their only hope of penetrating into Black's position is along the f-file. Naturally, Karpov makes sure that this hope is frustrated. Assuming that White can do nothing aggressive, how should Black play to increase his advantage? Karpov answers this question in the course of his subsequent play.

25 ... a5!

First, Black threatens 26...a4 which would undermine the c-pawn. It would be a fixed target and White would no longer be able to defend it safely with b2-b3. After 26...a4, Black would also have the option of ...♖a5 followed by ...♗f6 and ...♖h5, bringing his rook into the attack.

26 b3

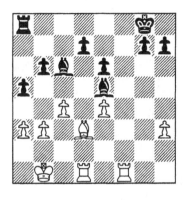

Now 26...a4? could be answered by 27 b4, keeping the black rook out of a5. The pawn on a4 would also be a target - if the rook moves away, then ♗c2 followed by b4-b5 would threaten to win the pawn. However, in playing 26 b3, White has compromised his pawn structure somewhat on the queenside. This slight weakness proves crucial later on.

26 ... d6!!

A wonderful example of Karpov's positional play. He realises that the bishop on c6 should go to g6 in order to thwart any white activity on the f-file. And by moving from c6, the way is cleared for the rook to enter into the game via c8, c5 and eventually h5. This is planning on a grand scale!

27 ♖d2 ♗e8
28 ♔c2 ♗g6
29 ♖df2

The rooks may look impressive, but there is no breakthrough square. Karpov's subtle play has reduced his opponent to passivity. He now continues his plan.

| 29 | ... | ♖c8 |
| 30 | ♔d1 | ♗d4! |

The rook must move away from the f-file since 31 ♖f3? ♗h5 or 31 ♖f4 ♗e3 32 ♖h4 ♗g5 win the exchange.

| 31 | ♖a2 | ♖c5 |

Now that the white rook has been forced away from f2, this can be played without allowing 32 ♖f8 mate.

| 32 | ♖g2 |

All White can do is mark time and defend against any direct threats.

| 32 | ... | ♖h5 |
| 33 | ♖f3 | ♗e8! |

Now that his rook has been activated, Black begins the next phase of his plan. This involves utilising his kingside pawn majority.

34	♔c2	g6
35	♗e2	♖e5
36	♗d3	♔g7
37	♖g4	g5

Karpov is finally happy with his preparations and the pawns begin to advance.

| 38 | ♖f1 | ♗c5 |
| 39 | ♔b2 |

Here Karpov recommends 39 a4. However, White's pawns then lose their flexibility on the queenside, and he has no hope of ever activating his game with b3-b4.

| 39 | ... | ♗g6 |
| 40 | h4 |

Lutz decides to force the issue.

If he waits with 40 ♖g3 then 40...h6 41 ♖g4 ♗e3 followed by ...♗f4 wins the e-pawn. However, Karpov would probably have chosen a slower, more methodical plan of execution.

| 40 | ... | gxh4 |
| 41 | ♖xh4 | ♖g5 |

As Karpov points out 41...d5! is decisive after 42 ♖ff4 (42 ♖e1 ♗f2) 42...♗e3 43 ♖fg4 ♗f2 44 ♖h2 ♗d4+ followed by ...dxe4. After winning the e-pawn and creating his own passed pawn on e4, Black could gradually plan the advance of the h7 pawn. White would not have the resources to fight off both passed pawns. However, Karpov's 41...♖g5 is also ultimately winning.

42	♖h2	♖g3
43	♗c2	♗d4+
44	♔c1	a4!

Breaking up White's queenside pawns. Compare the note after White's 26th move.

45 bxa4 ♖xa3 46 ♔d2 ♖g3 47 ♗d3 ♖g5 48 ♖fh1 ♗e5 49 ♖h3 ♗d4 50 ♖3h2 ♖g3 51 ♖f1 ♗f6 52 ♖b1 ♗g5+ 53 ♔c2 ♗e3 54 ♖a1 ♗g1 55 ♖d2 ♔f6

After interminable manoeuvres, designed no doubt to demoralise his opponent, Karpov brings his king into the centre in order to pressurise White's defences even further. There is also the looming threat from the h-pawn, which White will find very hard to stop.

56 a5 bxa5 57 ♖xa5 ♗c5 58

♖a1 ♔e5 59 ♖f1 ♗g1 60 ♖dd1

This loses control of the second rank, but White had to do something against Black's plan of advancing his h-pawn.

60...♗e3 61 ♖f8

An aggressive move, but what is there to attack?

61...♖g2+ 62 ♔b3 ♖h2!

Black wants to play ...♗h5, activating his bishop and driving the white rook away from the good defensive square at d1, without allowing ♖h1 in reply.

63 ♗b1 ♗h5 64 ♖e1 ♗f2 65 ♖f1 ♗c5 66 ♖e1 ♗e2 67 ♗a2

White loses more and more ground.

67...♖h3+ 68 ♔b2 ♗a3+ 69 ♔a1 ♗d3 70 ♗b1

This allows a winning combination. However, the game could not be saved. Even if White survived direct threats to his king (for example, 70 ♖g8 ♗b4 71 ♖c1 ♖h1!! 72 ♖xh1 ♗c3 mate) the h-pawn would prove unstoppable. It's curious that Karpov never needs to use this pawn in the game.

70...♗b4 71 ♖c1 ♗d2 72 ♖d1

72 ♗xd3 ♗xc1 is hopeless despite the opposite coloured bishops. The h-pawn runs through.

72...♗c3+ 73 ♔a2 ♗xc4+ 74 ♔a3 ♗e2 0-1

White was probably relieved to be able to resign. Wherever his rook goes, it will be lost to a discovered attack, e.g. 75 ♖c1 ♗d2+. A fine display of sustained pressure from Karpov.

Sion Castro-Karpov
Lyon 1993

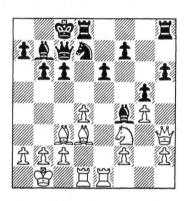

White has just played 18 ♗c3. He hopes that the threat of 19 d5, discovering an attack on the rook on h8, will force Black either to abandon the defence of the h-pawn or weaken himself in some other way. Karpov, however, sticks to the principle that the best answer to a threat is to ignore it. He played:

18   ...   ♔b8!

White had the temerity to call Karpov's bluff with

19   d5   cxd5
20   ♗xh8   ♖xh8

Already, we can discern some similar features to the Lutz-Karpov game above. Black has a strong dark-squared bishop which has no rival. This gives him ascendancy over some key central squares such as e5, f4 and c5. (However, the domination is not as great as in the Lutz game.) The white rooks have no open lines.

Their plight is even worse than in the Lutz game, where they at least had the f-file. If White tries to open lines with c2-c4 then the bishop on b7 will become very strong after ...dxc4. Besides, the square c1 is controlled by Black's bishop so it is not clear that White would be able to profit by the opening of the c-file. The alternative method of opening a file is h2-h4, but there are great practical difficulties in achieving this advance. (The game continuation will make this clear.) Assuming that c2-c4 is unwise and h2-h4 impractical, White has no plan. All he can do is wait and see if Black can improve his position.

21 ♘d4 a6!

Not 21...♗xh2 22 ♘b5 ♕f4 23 ♖h1 winning the bishop. But now 22...♗xh2 is threatened.

22 ♘xe6

'Patience' - 22 ♕f1 ♘c5 23 h3 ♖c8 - leaves White without any constructive ideas. Black can prepare to advance his centre pawns and drive back White's pieces. Having watched the slow and excruciating demise of Lutz, one cannot be too critical of Sion's decision.

22 ... fxe6

23 ♖xe6 ♘e5

Although White has nominal material compensation, the two minor pieces far outweigh the rook and pawns. White's rook on d1 is still passive and his kingside pawns are weak. If, for example, White plays 24 ♖xh6 then

24...♖xh6 25 ♕xh6 ♘xg4 26 ♕h8+ ♔a7 and White will lose one or more of his kingside pawns, e.g. 27 f3 ♘f2 (best) 28 ♖e1 ♘xd3 29 cxd3 ♗xh2. In trying to prevent the dislocation of his kingside, Sion falls under a direct mating attack.

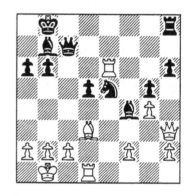

24 ♗f5 ♘c4

25 ♖xh6

If 25 ♖de1 ♕c5! with ideas of ...♕b4 or ...♕d4 or ...♕xf2.

25 ... ♖xh6

26 ♕xh6 ♕e5!

A powerful entrance, threatening mate. The position of Black's queen and bishop may remind the reader of the Lutz game.

27 ♕f8+ ♔a7

28 ♕b4 ♘d2+!

Once again Karpov demonstrates that he is a masterly tactician.

29 ♔a1 ♕e2

Now the rook has no good squares. 30 ♖c1 ♘b3+ or 30 ♖h1 d4 fail to solve his problems.

30 ♖g1 ♕xf2

31 ♖d1 ♕e2

Back again, with one white pawn less.

| 32 | ♖g1 | ♕xh2 |
| 33 | ♖d1 | ♕e2 |

Ditto.

| 34 | ♖h1 | |

Now at last the rook sees daylight, but it's too late.

| 34 | ... | a5 |
| 35 | ♕c3 | |

An understandable blunder after all that White has been through. Karpov gives 35 ♕f8 ♘c4 followed by 36...♕e5 or 36...♗e5. White's king wouldn't last long against the combined force of Black's minor pieces. (The same plan would apply if White had played 34 ♖g1.) In a middlegame-type position involving a direct attack on a king, two minor pieces are generally of much more value than a rook. If we remove the queens in this position, White's chances are greatly improved.

| 35 | ... | d4 |
| | 0-1 | |

Yes, Karpov is a mean player who loves to torture his opponent.

8 Queen for Rook and Bishop Sacrifices

To the beginner, the loss of the queen is almost as devastating as the loss of the king. Perhaps this is why players often miss the chance to make an effective queen sacrifice: they never quite overcome their early impression of the queen's omnipotence.

Here are some examples to persuade the reader that it can be a good idea to part with the queen. The examples are grouped in descending order, from the brilliant to the bad.

8.1 Completely winning

Vulevic-Regez
Wettingen 1993

(see following diagram)

Here Black played 22...♖xb2 23 ♘xd5 ♗xd5. One cannot call this a 'real' sacrifice - it is a simplifying combination, after which the queen cannot prevent the rook and bishop shepherding home the b-pawn. The game finished 24 ♕xh5 ♖xg2+ 25 ♔f1 e6 (the rook on g2 thwarts White's last hope,

perpetual check) 26 ♕h4 b2 27 ♕d8+ ♔g7 28 ♕xb6 ♖xh2 and White resigned since ...♖h1+ followed by queening is an unstoppable threat.

No fine judgement was needed in this case. Indeed, the finish could be calculated from 22...♖xb2 to 28...♖xh2, in view of the forced nature of the play.

8.2 Winning

Reeh-Lau
Germany 1993

(see following diagram)

Here White played:

20   ♕xc7!   ♖xc7
21   ♖xc7

We note the following features of the sacrifice:

i) The rook infiltrates to the seventh rank, where it is excellently placed. Black cannot contest control of the open c-file - the only open line on the whole board.

ii) The power of the bishop on a3 is greatly increased by the disappearance of Black's dark-squared bishop. The dark squares in Black's kingside are indefensible. Meanwhile, the black bishop on b7 is a miserable piece.

iii) *Black has absolutely no counterplay.* His queen is blocked in by the pawn structure on the kingside. White's position contains no chinks. The king on g1 is perfectly safe in its fortress. The question of counterplay and king safety will come up again and again in our discussion of queen sacrifices. Black would willingly give up one or two pawns or even

a piece to get an attack on the white king in this position; but there is no possibility at all here. Meanwhile, White has a clear and simple plan to increase his advantage. He can put his bishop on e5 and double rooks on the seventh rank.

21   ...   ♗c8
22   ♗e7   ♕f7
23   ♗b5

The bishops flex their power.

23   ...   ♗d7
24   ♗d6   ♖d8

The valiant 24...♗xb5 comes out a piece down.

25   ♗e5

Finally the bishop reaches its ideal square. White is in no hurry to play ♖xa7.

25   ...   ♕e8
26   ♗a6   ♖a8
27   ♗b7   ♖b8
28   ♗a6   ♖a8 .

A bit of cat and mouse. Now White begins the final stage of his plan - to play his knight to c5, threatening to capture the bishop followed by ♖bb7, crashing through on the seventh rank.

29   ♘b3!   ♘c4
30   ♗xc4   dxc4
31   ♘c5

White has carefully calculated that his attack gets in before Black can set up any threats along the newly opened a8-h1 diagonal. It is frustrating for Black's bishop that it sees daylight too late. After 31...♗c6 32 ♖g7+ ♔f8 33 ♖h7! Black loses his queen to the threat of 34

♖h8+. The black queen is so constricted that it has no safe square to flee to.

31	...	♖d8
32	♗f6	♖b8
33	♖xb8	♕xb8
34	♖b7!	♕f8
35	♘xd7	♕a3

Or 35...♕f7 36 ♖b8+ mating.

| 36 | ♘e5 | ♕f8 |
| 37 | ♖g7+ | 1-0 |

It was possible for White to make the queen sacrifice above without any concrete calculation at all. The following one required more calculation, though again it is positional in nature.

G.Kuzmin-Turov
Russia 1993

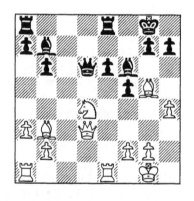

| 20 | ... | ♗e4 |

Here Black saw that 20...♗xd4 21 ♕xf5! or 20...♕xd4 (which is best) 21 ♖xe6! ♖xe6 (21...♕xd3 22 ♖xe8 mate is the simplest queen sacrifice in this book) 22 ♗xe6+ ♔h8 23 ♕xf5 is in White's favour. So rather than recapture the piece Black played this *zwischenzug*, trustingly attacking White's queen. White's reply was unexpected:

| 21 | ♗xf6! | ♗xd3 |
| 22 | ♗e5 | |

White only has two pieces for the queen, but Black's queen has no safe square. For example, if 22...♕d7 then 23 ♖ad1 ♗e4 24 ♘xe6! tears Black apart; or 22...♕c5 23 ♘xe6 ♖xe6 24 ♗xe6+ ♔h8 25 ♖ac1 ♕e7 26 ♖c7! ♕xe6 27 ♗xg7+ and wins. This last variation demonstrates the enormous power of the two bishops bearing down on Black's king position.

| 22 | ... | ♕e7! |
| 23 | ♖ac1! | |

Black hoped for 23 ♘xe6 when 23...♕xe6! 24 ♗xe6+ ♖xe6 gives a drawn position. White correctly judges that his attack is worth more than the queen. Now, 23...♖ac8? would lose a rook after 24 ♖xc8 and 25 ♗xe6+. Meanwhile 24 ♖c7 is threatened. So Black decided to give up a rook to at least be free of one of his tormentors, the knight on d4.

23	...	♖ad8
24	♘c6	♕xh4
25	♘xd8	♖xd8

25...♕xd8 26 ♖ed1 is a fatal pin.

| 26 | ♗xe6+ | ♔h8 |
| 27 | ♖c7 | |

The idea of a dominant rook on c7 and raking bishops should recall the previous game to the reader.

27	...	♕h6
28	♖xa7!	

Don't hurry! Before winning back the queen, White snaffles a pawn.

28	...	♗e4
29	♗xg7+	♕xg7
30	♖xg7	♔xg7

and White has a winning endgame. The game finished:

31 f3 ♔f6 32 ♗a2 ♗a8 33 ♖e6+ ♔g5 34 ♖xb6 ♖d1+ 35 ♔h2 ♖d2 36 ♔h3 ♖d1 37 ♖b4 ♖d2 38 ♗e6 ♔f6 39 ♖b6 ♔g5 40 ♖b5 ♔f4 41 ♖xf5+ ♔e3 42 ♔g3 ♖xb2 43 ♖e5+ 1-0

8.3   Promising

Lautier-M.Gurevich
Munich 1993

Black played:

38	...	♕xd3!
39	♕xd3	♖xe3
40	♕d2	

In return for the queen, Black has a good co-ordination of the pieces. The white pawn on a3 is defenceless, and after it is captured, Black will have a tremendously powerful a-pawn. This pawn can be forced to its queening square by the knight and bishop, while the rooks tie White down in the centre, assuming of course that nothing happens in the meantime.

White's one hope is the slight weakness of Black's king position, especially the g6 square. Note that in the previous example, there were no weaknesses whatsoever in the queen sacrificers position. This meant he could manoeuvre as he pleased without any risk at all. Note that if Black's king were on h8 and the Black h-pawn on h7, White would be lost. He would have no counterplay.

Here, however, he must tread carefully. For example, if Black now played 40...♘xa3, White could respond 41 f5! g5 42 f6! (activity at all costs!) 42...♘xf6 43 ♘g3 and White has attacking chances. Since the a-pawn is doomed anyway, Black tried to reduce his opponent's counterplay before capturing it by returning the knight to the centre (with the threat of ...♘g4):

40	...	♘f6
41	♗f1	♘xa3?

In *Informator 57*, Gurevich criticises his decision and instead recommends 41...♖xa3! 42 ♘g3 ♖a1 43 ♔g2 a3 44 ♗d3 (44 ♗c4 is met by ...♘c7 and ...♘cd5)

44...a2 with a clear advantage to Black. Now White has a chance:

42	♘g3	♖e1
43	♔g2	♘g4
44	♗e2!	♘xf2
45	♕xe1	♘g4
46	♕d2	♘e3+
47	♔f2	♘d5

Now White succeeds in eliminating the dangerous passed pawn since 48...♘c3 49 ♕d7 followed by ♗d3 or f4-f5 gives White an attack.

48	...	♘xf4
49	♕xa4	♘b1
50	♕d1!	

Lautier agrees to enter an endgame with another material imbalance rather than face the dangerous all-out attack of Black's pieces after 50 ♕c2 ♘c3 followed by ...♗d4+.

50	...	♘c3
51	♕d7	♖xe2+
52	♘xe2	♘fxe2
53	b5?	

As Gurevich points out, 53 ♕xb7 ♘d4 is only slightly better for Black. Black's plan would be to win the two white queenside pawns for his own c-pawn and then advance his own kingside pawns, sheltering his king with his minor pieces. · Whether he could win or not is uncertain, but it will certainly be a long and arduous defence for White.

53	...	♘d4!
54	bxc6	

54 b6 loses to 54...♘e4+ and 55...♘xc5.

54	...	bxc6

55	♔g2	♘d5
56	h4	

This makes the win easier since the pawn becomes a target on h4. Black now proceeded to win first the c-pawn then the h-pawn:

56...h5 57 ♔h3 ♘f4+ 58 ♔h2 ♘fe6 59 ♕e7 ♔h6 60 ♔h1 ♗f8 61 ♕f6 ♗g7 62 ♕e7 ♘f8 63 ♕e3 ♔h7 64 ♕e8 ♔g8 65 ♔g2 ♗f6 66 ♔h3 ♘de6! 67 ♕xc6 ♗d4 68 ♕d5 ♗xc5 69 ♕b7 ♗d4 70 ♕d5 ♔h7 71 ♕f3 ♗g7 72 ♕f7 ♘d4 73 ♔g2 ♘fe6 74 ♔h3 ♘c5 75 ♕e7 ♘d3 76 ♕e3 ♘e6! 77 ♔g3 ♘e5 78 ♕b6 ♘f8 79 ♕d6 ♘f7 80 ♕e7 ♗e5+ 81 ♔h3 ♔g7 82 ♔g2 ♘h7 83 ♔h3 ♘f6 84 ♕e6 ♘g8 0-1

Black has finally reached his ideal set-up. He will play ...♘g8-h6-f5 and ...♗f6 winning the h-pawn. Then the advance of his passed pawns will be decisive.

Klovans-Didysko
Katowice 1993

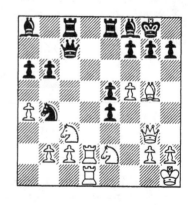

White has sacrificed a pawn and now tried to force home his attack with:

26   &f6!?

This threatens 27 &xg7! followed by 28 f6, mating. So Black defended with:

26   ...   &h8

White then pressed on with:

27   &d7

This looks decisive. If 27...&c4 then 28 b3 &c6 29 &xf7 gxf6 30 &dd7 and mate beckons on h7, unless Black sacrifices his queen. Black in fact did so straight away:

27   ...   gxf6!
28   &xc7   &xc7

White's attack has vanished. All Black's pieces are excellently co-ordinated and his bishops are potent. In trying to gain some central squares for his knights, by capturing the e-pawn, White unfortunately brings Black's bishops to life.

29   &h4   &e7
30   &xe4   &g8!

Better than 30...&c4 31 &2g3 &g8 32 &d7! with an attack. Now Black has strong pressure against g2.

31   c3

31 &d6 &xg2! 32 &xf7+ &g8 33 &h6+ &g7 wins, or alternatively 31 &xf6 &g7! threatening both 32...&xg2+ and 32...&c6 winning the knight.

31   ...   &d5

Threatening 32...&e3 and 33...&g4.

32   &2g3   &f4

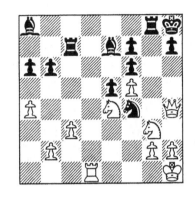

33   &f1

Didysko criticises this move in *Informator 57* without saying what White should play. Black is threatening 33...&c4, so what should White do?

a) 33 b3 (preventing ...&c4) &xc3! 34 &xc3 &xg2+ 35 &g1 &c5+ 36 &d4 &xd4 mate.

b) 33 &d6 &c4 34 &xf6 &xg2+ 35 &g1 &h3+ wins White's queen and remains a rook up.

c) 33 &xf6 &g7 34 &h6 (hoping to play 35 &xg7+ and 36 &e8+ winning both rooks) 34...&xg2+ 35 &g1 &c5+ and wins.

d) 33 &e1 &c4 threatening 34...&d3 35 &e2 &xg3! 36 hxg3 &xe4 planning a fork on f2.

To sum up: White is probably losing even before 33 &f1.

33   ...   &c4
34   &xf4

Equally useless is 34 &e1 &d3 as in line (d) above.

34   ...   exf4
35   &xf4   &xg3!

| 36 | hxg3 | ♗xe4 |
| 37 | ♔h2 | |

Of course 37 b3 ♗xg2+ loses. What follows is White's death throes, as his queen is gradually overwhelmed by the numerous black pieces:

37... ♗d5 38 ♕b8+ ♔g7 39 ♕xb6 ♖xa4 40 ♕c7 ♖e4 41 ♕a5 ♗c4 42 ♕c7 ♗f1 43 ♔g1 ♗d3 44 ♕d7 ♗c5+ 45 ♔h2 ♗e2 46 ♕c6 ♖e5

| 47 | g4 | |

Black threatened 47...♗g4, 48...♖xf5 and 49...♖h5 mate, so White makes space for the king.

| 47 | ... | ♗f2 |

Now there are ideas of 48...♖e3 and 49...♗g3+ with a quick mate on the back rank.

| 48 | g5 | fxg5 |
| 49 | g4 | ♗xg4 |

A good harvest.

50	♕xa6	♖e2
51	f6+	♔h6
52	♕a8	

Its too late to do anything with the queenside pawns.

52	...	♗c5+
53	♔g3	♗h5
54	♕d5	♗e3
	0-1	

It's mate after 55...♗f4+, 56...g4+ and 57...♖h2.

A drastic defeat. Looking at the position after 30...♖g8, the punishment seemed out of all proportion to White's 'crimes'. Yet Black not only gained a healthy rook, bishop and pawn for the queen - the full theoretical mate-

rial equivalent - he also had many positional features in his favour: the open g-file for his rook bearing down on g2 where its power interacts with the enormously strong bishop on a8; a strong solid centre; a well placed knight on b4 which was easily manoeuvred to the even better c4 square; and, not least, the c4 square for his rook. His king was perfectly safe, and the black bishop on e7 hindered any attempt to break through on f6. Meanwhile, White's knights proved the adage that the worst bishop is better than the best knight!

8.4   Unclear

Genov-S.Ivanov
Berlin 1993

White has sacrificed a pawn for attacking chances. He must now have expected Black to move his queen (since 18 ♗h7+ followed by 19 ♖xd5 is threatened) when he has dangerous possibilities. In *Informator 58*, Ivanov gives the variation 17...♕a5 18 ♕e4! g6 19 ♕f4 ♔h7 20 ♗xg6+! ♔xg6 (20...fxg6 21 ♖d7+ followed by 22 ♕xh6 wins) 21 ♕f6+ ♔h7 22 ♖d3 with the threat of 23 ♘g5+! hxg5 24 ♖h3+ and mates.

Instead, Black killed the White attack stone dead by sacrificing his queen:

17	...	♖ad8!
18	♗h7+	♔xh7
19	♖xd5	♖xd5

Black now has active pieces, a solid pawn structure and a safe king. Furthermore, he has the theoretical material equivalent of a queen - a rook, bishop and pawn - so it is not clear that the term sacrifice is justified.

What should White do? At present, he cannot hope to directly attack Black's king by advancing his kingside pawns, since the bishop on b7 is waiting to gun him down along the a8-h1 diagonal if he loosens his position too much; for example, 20 g4 ♔g8 21

g5 ♖fd8 22 gxh6 ♘xe5! 23 ♘xe5 (23 ♕g3 ♘xf3+ 24 ♕xf3 ♖g5+ also loses for White) 23...♖d1+ and mates. Therefore White must be more subtle. He should probe with his queen and try to coax Black into weakening pawn advances.

Black, for his part, is in something of a dilemma. He has a very secure position and can draw by sitting tight. White is unable to puncture holes in his position. On the other hand, Black thinks he has winning chances by advancing his queenside pawns and creating a passed pawn. Such a policy is not without danger, as the game continuation demonstrates.

| 20 | h4 |

This is not the prelude to an unsound kingside attack. White is making an escape square for his king.

| 20 | ... | ♔g8 |

Preparatory to 21...♖fd8; Black defends the f-pawn. There is one chink in Black's armour and that is the insecure position of the knight on c6, which isn't defended by a pawn. Therefore 20...♖d7! preparing to manoeuvre the knight to the unassailable d5 square looks best. Then if 21 ♕a4 ♖fd8 22 ♖c1 ♘e7 and 23 ♕xa7? is impossible because of 23...♗xf3 in reply. Or if 21 ♖c1 immediately then 21...♘e7 and Black has nothing to fear. In the game, Black prefers to keep his rook on d5 and the knight on c6 in order to pressurise the e5 pawn. But this gives White some chances to pressurise the queenside.

21	♖c1	♖fd8
22	♕a4	♖a5
23	♕b3	♖ad5

Black has managed to fend off White's first attempt to promote a weakness in his queenside. Note that 23...♘xe5 24 ♘xe5 ♖xe5 25 ♖c7 ♗d5 26 ♕c3 is bad for Black. The exchange of Black's a-pawn for White's e-pawn would loosen the cohesion of Black's queenside and rid White of his weak e-pawn.

24	♔h2	♖8d7
25	♖c3	b5!?

25...♘xe5 26 ♘xe5 ♖xe5 27 ♕a4 attacks the d7 rook and so wins the a-pawn; after the plausible 27...♖ed5 28 ♕xa7 White has achieved a queenside breakthrough, leaving the b6 pawn very vulnerable. 25...b5!? hopes to turn the queenside pawns into a positive asset, not just an object of attack. But any advance is double-edged.

26	♕c2!	

The insecure position of the knight reveals itself again. Now 26...♘xe5 27 ♘xe5 ♖xe5 28 ♖c8+! won't do.

26	...	♘b4
27	♕e2	a5 (D)
28	♕e3!	

The queen finds a way to slip into the black position via the squares left unprotected by Black's queenside pawn advances; in particular, b6 beckons. To achieve this, White has to give up his a-pawn for Black's, but this isn't necessarily a disadvantageous exercise, as will be seen.

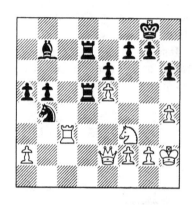

28	...	♘xa2
29	♖a3	♘b4
30	♖xa5	

Both sides have made progress. Black has eliminated White's last queenside pawn. This is an important achievement since we know that a queen plus a passed pawn is a dangerous combination. Furthermore, Black's own passed pawn could become an important feature if he succeeds in advancing it; but this would be difficult. White has succeeded in activating his rook on an open file and his queen is also ready to infiltrate into the black position. If White managed to penetrate to the back rank, then Black's king would find itself in danger. However, Black has adequate play.

30	...	♘c6
31	♖a2	♘d4

If 31...b4 then 32 ♕b6 threat-

ens 33 ♖c2.

32 ♖a7

Here 32 ♘xd4 ♖xd4 leaves the h-pawn hard to defend since 33 g3 ♖d1, threatening mate, is dangerous.

32 ... ♘xf3+?!

Evidently a winning attempt. Black should prefer 32...♘c6! when White has nothing better than 33 ♖a2 ♘d4 with a draw by repetition.

33 ♕xf3 b4
34 ♕e2!

An excellent move. Now 34...♖d4 35 ♕b5 or 34...b3 35 ♕c4 b2 36 ♖xb7! (Ivanov) are unsatisfactory. So Black must tread carefully.

34 ... ♖c5
35 ♖a4 ♖d4
36 ♖a7 ♖xh4+?!

A lunch under dangerous conditions, as Nimzowitsch would have said. Ivanov points out that 36...♗e4 37 ♕h5 ♗g6 is better. White could also answer 36...♗e4 with 37 ♕e3 when the battle continues.

37 ♔g3 ♖e4
38 ♕d1! ♖d5

Here 38...♗d5 39 ♕h5 g6 40 ♕xh6 ♖xe5 was unclear according to Ivanov. In fact, White has chances with 41 ♖xf7! ♔xf7 42 ♕h7+ ♔f8 (42...♔f6 43 ♕h8+ ♔f5? 44 ♕f8+ leads to mate in two) 43 ♕h8+ ♔f7 44 ♕xe5; however after 44...b3 the passed pawn should save Black.

39 ♕b1

Black must give up his bishop.

39 ... ♖exe5

Ivanov also mentions 39...♖b5 40 ♖xb7 ♖xb7 41 ♕xe4 ♖b8. However, this sacrifice seems to fail. White plays 42 ♕d4 b3 43 ♕b2 followed by placing his king on b1; then his queen is freed to chase away the black rook from the b-file when the b-pawn can be captured. Or the queen can be used in combination with kingside pawn advances to capture one or more of Black's kingside pawns.

(analysis diagram)

A sample variation: 43...♔h7 44 ♔f3 ♔g8 45 ♔e3 ♔h7 46 ♔d2 ♔g8 47 ♔c1 g6 (this vacates g7 and thus makes it possible to defend f7 with the king if White's queen forces the rook away from the second rank) 48 ♔b1 ♔g7 49 ♕d4 b2 50 ♕d6 ♖b7 51 f4 ♔g8 52 g4 ♔g7 53 ♕c6 and the rook has to leave the second rank, as if the b-pawn goes, Black is lost. So:

a) 53...♖b4 54 f5 gxf5 (54...♖xg4 55 f6+ and 56 ♕e8 wins) 55 gxf5 exf5 56 e6! (threatening ♕c3+) 56...♖e4 57 ♕xe4! followed by 58 e7 wins.

b) 53...♖b3 54 f5 gxf5 55 gxf5 exf5 56 ♕f6+ ♔g8 57 e6! ♖b7 58 ♕d7+ and 59 e7 wins.

c) 53...♖b8 54 f5 gxf5 55 gxf5 exf5 56 e6! followed by 57 e7 wins as 56...fxe6? loses the rook.

| 40 | ♖xb7 | ♖b5 |
| 41 | ♖c7 | ♖ec5! |

Now that the e5 pawn has been eliminated, Black can sacrifice his b-pawn and still achieve a draw. The game continuation will demonstrate that Black can set up an impenetrable fortress on the kingside.

42 ♖xc5 ♖xc5 43 ♕xb4 ♖f5 44 ♕b8+ ♔h7 45 ♕f8 h5 46 f3 ♔g6 47 ♕h8 ♖d5 48 ♔h4 ♖f5 49 ♕b8 ♖d5 50 ♕b1+ ♔h6 51 ♕c1+ ♔g6 52 ♕e3 ♖f5

| 53 | g4 | |

After his fruitless manoeuvres, White realises that only pawn advances can hope to break through. The black rook pivots

between the d5 and f5 squares, so 53 g4, taking away f5, looks right.

53	...	hxg4
54	fxg4	♖d5
55	♕f4	♖a5!

It turns out that the rook has safe, albeit unprotected squares.

| 56 | ♕e4+ | ♔h6 |
| 57 | ♕f3 | f6 |

Black could also play 57...♔g6 58 ♕d3+ ♔h6 59 ♕d2+ g5+! with a draw.

58	♕e3	♖g5
59	♕xe6	♔h7
½-½		

Now the black rook can oscillate forever between e5 and g5 and White cannot break through. A very instructive game.

8.5 Unpromising

Korchnoi-Stean
London 1980

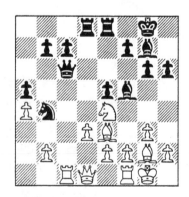

Black has played the opening poorly and now finds himself under intense pressure on the queenside. If his queen retreats to d7 then 19 ♘c5 will win the b-pawn for nothing. Other queen moves allow 20 ♖xc7. Therefore Stean decides to sacrifice his queen for rook and bishop, and trust in the solidity of his position. This is undoubtedly the best course of action, since all alternatives are completely hopeless.

18 ...   ♗xe4
19 ♖xc6   ♗xc6

At first glance, things do not look too bad for Black. All his pieces are well developed, his king is safe, and there are no obvious pawn weaknesses in his position. The knight on b4 seems excellently placed to obstruct any White attack on the queenside pawns. However, the game continuation proves that Black's queenside pawn structure is fatally weak. Imagine if a genie appeared at the chessboard and gave Black three extra 'positional' moves. He would use them wisely to play ...♗xg2, ...b7-b6 and ...c7-c5. Then assuming we have allowed White to play ♔xg2, we would reach the following position *(D)*:

Black no longer has any worries. His queenside is rock solid. There is no way that the b6 pawn can be attacked. If the white queen landed on b5, Black could simply play ...♖d6. Nor has White any hope of a breakthrough on the kingside. There are no weak points to attack there, and a move like f4 would

only weaken White's centre position. This then is the set-up Black is aiming for after 19...♗xc6. He cannot really hope for supernatural intervention, but if White potters about for the next couple of moves, then he will have time to carry out his plan of securing the queenside from attack.

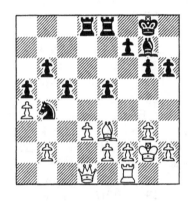

(analysis diagram)

20   ♕c1!

Unfortunately Korchnoi is not a player to potter around. 20 ♕c1 threatens 21 ♗xh6 so Black has not got time to carry out his consolidating plan above.

20   ...   h5
21   ♗xc6   ♘xc6

The knight, temporarily at least, has to relinquish the b4 square, since 21...bxc6 ruins the pawn structure.

22   ♕c4!

Now we see the point of Korchnoi's plan beginning with 20 ♕c1. He homes in on the weak b7 pawn before Black has the chance to play ...b7-b6 and ...c7-c5.

| 22 | ... | ♖e6 |

Bolstering c6.

23	♖c1	b6
24	♕b5	♖dd6
25	♕a6!	

Threatening to win the c-pawn with 26 ♕c8+. Black has no good defence. For example, 25...♖e7 26 ♖xc6! ♖xc6 27 ♕a8+ wins; or 25...♔h7 26 ♕b7 and the pawn falls.

25	...	♘d4
26	♕c8+	♔h7
27	♗xd4	exd4
28	♖xc7	

Now Black's game crumbles. There is no hope of a blockade on the queenside. If now 28...♖xe2 29 ♖xf7 threatens 30 ♕f8.

28	...	♖f6
29	♕b7	♖de6
30	♔f1!	1-0

Simplest. Black is denied any counterplay at all. Now 30...♔g8 31 ♖xf7! ♖xf7 32 ♕c8+ wins back a rook with an easily winning position.

8.6   Conclusion

What conclusions can we draw from our examination of queen for rook and bishop sacrifices?

To be effective, the player with the rook and bishop must have:

i) A safe king (absolutely essential).

ii) A solid pawn structure with no chinks.

iii) A well co-ordinated and self-defending force.

Also, the queen works very well with passed pawns. In fact, a queen and passed pawns often overcome a much larger army.

These are of course only general rules. As always, the important thing is to examine the individual position in front of you and decide whether in the specific circumstances the sacrifice is sound.

9   It's Your Turn

The reader is invited to examine 20 positions taken from recent master games. Imagine you are the player to move. Ask yourself:

i) What are the important features of the position (for example, a safe king, a strong centre or a weak pawn structure)? Are my pieces well co-ordinated? What about my opponent's pieces?

ii) Do I stand better or worse? What is my correct plan?

iii) Can I make a positional sacrifice to implement this plan?

(Become aware of the tactical features of the position, e.g. a queen and rook separated by the distance of a knight fork - can this be exploited?)

iv) If possible, is the positional sacrifice tactically sound? Is it equal, good or winning?

There are clear answers to most of the puzzles. However, one cannot expect complete clarity; otherwise we would be in the realm of combinations rather than positional sacrifices.

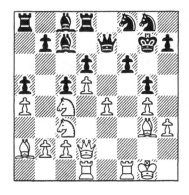

1. White to play

2. White to play

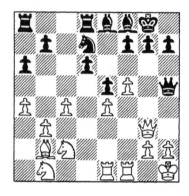

3. Black to play

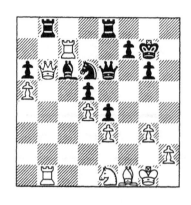

6. White to play

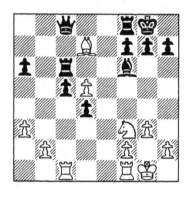

4. White to play

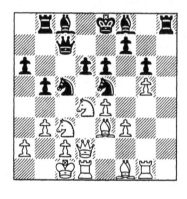

7. White to play

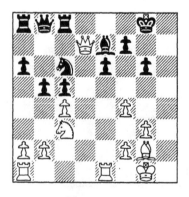

5. White to play

8. White to play

9. Black to play

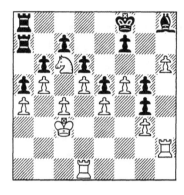

12. White to play

10. White to play

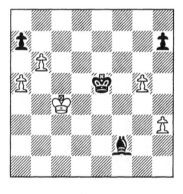

13. Black to play

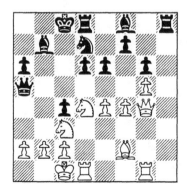

11. White to play

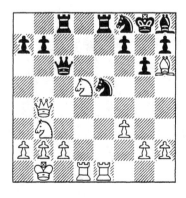

14. White to play

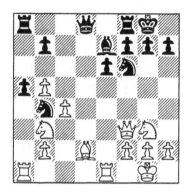

15. White to play

18. White to play

16. White to play

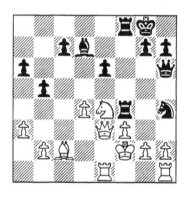

19. Black to play

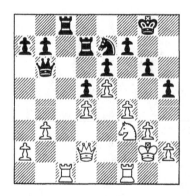

17. White to play

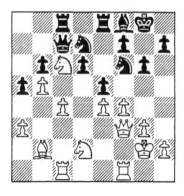

20. White to play

Answers

1. **24 e5!** is a thematic break-through. Now after 24...dxe5 25 d6 ♕e8 (25...♕d7 26 dxc7! ♕xd2 27 cxd8(♕)! wins) 26 ♕g2 ♗b8 27 ♘b6 ♖a6 (27...♖a7 28 ♘b5) 28 ♘xc8 ♖xc8 29 ♕xb7+ and wins. So Black tried **24...fxe5 25 ♘e4** (a beautiful square for the knight, vacated by 24 e5!) **25...h6** (preventing 26 ♘xg5) **26 ♘xe5!** and **Black resigned**. After 26...dxe5 (or 27 ♖f7+ wins) 27 d6 ♕e8 (27...♕d7 is the same) White has a choice of wins, e.g. 28 ♗xg8 ♔xg8 29 ♘f6+ or 28 ♖f7+ ♕xf7 29 ♗xf7 ♔xf7 30 ♕f2+ and 31 dxc7. (Glek-Dreyer, Hamburg 1993)

2. White in fact has a forced win: **45 ♖xa5! bxa5 46 ♖b7 ♕c8 47 ♖xf7+ ♔h8 48 ♕c1!** and mate next move cannot be averted. 1-0 (Maiwald-Masserey, Switzerland 1993)

3. There is no forced win here, but **21...b5!** undermines White's disorganised queenside. White did not want to be left with iso-lated pawns after 22...bxc4, so he accepted the offer: **22 cxb5 axb5 23 axb5 ♖a2 24 ♕c3**. This seems to hold things together. However, a second pawn sacrifice released all the stored up energy in Black's position: **24...d5! 25 exd5 ♘f6 26 ♘ba3** (26 ♖xe5

♘g4 or 26 ♕xe5 ♗d6) **26...e4 27 b4 ♖xd5 28 ♕b3** (trapping the rook on a2, but Black is so active that he gains a decisive kingside attack) **28...♖d3 29 ♕xa2 ♗d6 30 h3** (if 30 g3 ♗xg3 or 30...♖d2 gives a winning attack) **30...♖xh3+ 31 ♔g1 ♕h4!** (cutting off the king's escape) **White resigned** since 32 gxh3 ♕g3+ mates. (Müller-Hort, Germany 1994)

4. Should White capture the rook or the queen? Actually, there isn't much choice, since 20 ♗xc8 ♖cxc8 leaves White unable to save his d-pawn after 21...♖fd8. So White must make a virtue out of necessity and play **20 dxc6!**. After **20...♕c7 21 ♖xc5**. White has a rook, knight and strong passed pawn for the queen. Moreover, his position is solid, his king safe and his pieces well co-ordinated: all the criteria we adjudged necessary for a suc-cessful queen sacrifice in Chapter 8. Evidently there is more virtue than necessity about White's position. This does not of course mean that he must win, although in the game he did so: **21...♕d6 22 b4 g6 23 ♖d1 d3 24 ♗h3 ♗d8 25 ♘e5 d2 26 ♘c4** (one is reminded of Capablanca's adage that a passed pawn is either very strong or very weak; Black's passed pawn looked threatening but it lacked effective defence) **26...♕e7 27 ♖xd2 ♕e1+ 28 ♗f1 ♗b6 29 ♘xb6 ♕xd2 30 c7** and

Black resigned. (Van Wely-Jonsson, Iceland 1994)

5. The immediate 20 ♗xc6 ♖a7 is nothing for White (and don't imagine you can sacrifice your queen after 20 ♗xc6 ♖a7 21 ♕xa7 ♕xa7 22 cxb5 axb5 23 ♗xb5: we have the familiar rook, bishop and passed pawn for the queen, but the passed pawn is a weakling on a2, and Black can easily gain strong counterplay before it gets very far). We have already seen some effective exchange sacrifices on e6, and this is another example: **20 ♖xe6!**. Now if 20...fxe6 21 ♕xe6+ ♔f8 (21...♔g7 22 ♗xc6 attacks e7) 22 ♗d5 and wins - 22...♔e8 23 ♗xc6+. So Black tried **20...♖a7 21 ♖xg6+! fxg6** (21...♔f8 22 ♕h3 fxg6 23 ♕h8+ ♔f7 24 ♗d5 mate, or 21...♔h7 22 ♕h3+! ♔xg6 23 ♗e4+) **22 ♕e6+ ♔g7 23 ♗xc6**. For the exchange, White has two pawns with the promise of more. But more importantly, he has destroyed Black's pawn centre and opened up his king for attack. The game, Karpov-Topalov from Linares 1993, finished: **23...♖d8 24 cxb5 ♗f6 25 ♘e4 ♗d4 26 bxa6 ♕b6 27 ♖d1 ♕xa6 28 ♖xd4! ♖xd4 29 ♕f6+ ♔g8 30 ♕xg6+ ♔f8 31 ♕e8+ ♔g7 32 ♕e5+ ♔g8 33 ♘f6+ ♔f7 34 ♗e8+ ♔f8 35 ♕xc5+ ♕d6 36 ♕xa7 ♕xf6 37 ♗h5 ♖d2 38 b3 ♖b2 39 ♔g2 1-0**. A rather aggressive variant of the Karpovian exchange sacrifice!

6. Black has just played 32...♗b7-c6 exposing an attack on White's queen. Should White play 33 ♕xb8 or 33 ♖xc6? 33 ♕xb8 ♖xb8 34 ♖xb8 is two rooks for the queen, but after 34...♗b5 (Shirov) there are no immediate targets for White's rooks and Black has the makings of a kingside attack after the bishops are exchanged and he plays ...♘f5. So in the game Bareev-Shirov, Tilburg 1993, White correctly preferred to sacrifice his queen: **33 ♖xc6! ♖xb6 34 ♖bxb6**. An interesting decision. 34 axb6 gives White a strong passed pawn, but then 34...♕e7 35 ♖c7 ♕g5 followed, after the e-pawn is defended, by ...♘f5, leads to unclear play. Bareev prefers to bring both his rooks into play and keep Black tied up. **34...♖d8 35 ♘g2 ♕e7 36 ♗xa6 ♘f5 37 ♖c5** (preventing 37...♕a3) **37...♖h8** (Black strives for counterplay before the a-pawn begins to advance) **38 ♖b7 ♕b6 39 ♖b6 ♕g5 40 ♖xd5?**. White's last couple of moves have shown the uncertainty of time pressure, and now he commits a blunder. Shirov gives 40 ♘f4 (with the threat of 41 ♖xg6+!) 40...♖h6 41 ♖xd5 ♕e7 42 ♖b3 ♘xe3! 43 ♖ex3 g5 as unclear. **40...♕h5!**. Not only attacking h2 but also preparing to penetrate on d1 or f3. That is why White had to prevent this move with 40 ♘f4. **41 h4 ♕f3 42 ♖xf5**. Desperation. Otherwise his king's position crumbles. **42...gxf5 43**

罝b5 豐xg3 44 罝xf5 罝xh4 45
奧c8 罝g4 46 罝f2 罝g5 and **White
resigned**. 47...豐xe3 or 47...罝xa5
follows. As we remarked in the
introduction, often the decisive
factor is not the inherent strength
of the sacrifice, but rather how
well the player handles the resulting position.

7. White played **17 奧xb5+
axb5 18 ᑎdxb5**. The idea is noble: after the queen moves, say
18...豐c6, 19 ᑎxd6+ 奧xd6 20
豐xd6 豐xd6 21 罝xd6, White has
three passed pawns for a piece.
These outweigh the piece and the
tactics also favour White:
21...ᑎb7 (hoping for 22 罝b6
ᑎxf3) 22 奧d4!? ᑎxd6? 23 奧xe5
wins or 22...ᑎxf3 23 ᑎxh8 ᑎxd6
24 罝g3 traps the knight. However, White has overlooked a
tactic right at the beginning of her
combination: **18...ᑎcd3+! 19
含b1** (19 cxd3 罝xb5 and ...ᑎxf3
is threatened) **19...豐d7 20 f4
罝xb5 21 ᑎxb5 豐xb5 22 cxd3
ᑎc6** (but not 22...ᑎf3 23 豐c3!).
Black is at least equal. He has
avoided the exchange of queens,
so that White's passed pawns
cannot be utilised - they must
keep back to guard White's king.
Meanwhile, Black's centre is
'bomb proof'. In the game the
minor pieces proved more effective than the rooks: **23 罝h1 罝xh1
24 罝xh1 奧a6 25 罝d1 含d7 26
豐c3 奧e7 27 奧c1 d5! 28 豐g7** (a
dangerous adventure but 28 e5
ᑎb4 29 d4 would be very pas-

sive) **28...豐c5! 29 exd5?! ᑎd4**
(now White's queen cannot return to the defence of the king) **30
dxe6+ fxe6 31 豐e5 奧xd3+ 32
含a1 豐c3+ 33 奧b2 ᑎc2+ 34
含b1 ᑎe3+ 35 含a1 豐xe5 36
罝xd3+ 豐d5 37 罝xd5+ ᑎxd5 38
奧e5 奧d6 39 奧b2 ᑎxf4 40 奧f6
ᑎd5 0-1** (Arachamia-Kotronias,
Crete 1993). Another reminder
that you can't play positionally
unless you check all the tactical
details.

8. This position arose in Kas-
parov-Short, Novgorod 1994. The
world champion played **18 f5!**
opening lines and breaking up
Black's centre. **18...豐h6+**
(18...exf5 19 豐xd5+ 豐f7 20
豐xa8 豐xa2 21 罝a3 wins, or
18...豐xf5 19 罝f3 豐g6 20 罝xf8+
ᑎxf8 21 ᑎb6! wins a piece) **19
含b1 罝xf5 20 罝f3! 罝xf3 21 gxf3**.
Black is tied up. He cannot co-
ordinate his pieces, mainly due to
the looming threat of ᑎb6.
21...豐f6 22 奧h3 含f7 23 c4!.
Another blow from the winds that
undermines Black's centre. Kasparov continuously strives to
open the position. **23...dxc4**
(23...d4 24 f4! exf4 25 罝xd4 e5
26 豐d5+ and 27 豐xa8 wins a
piece; an aesthetic continuation:
18 f5!, 23 c4 and 24 f4!) **24 ᑎc3!
豐e7 25 豐c6 罝b8 26 ᑎe4 ᑎb6
27 ᑎg5+ 含g8 28 豐e4 g6 29
豐xe5 罝b7 30 罝d6 c3 31 奧xe6+
奧xe6 32 罝xe6 1-0**

9. White has a wretched pawn

structure - two sets of doubled pawns and another two isolated pawns - to worry about. However, he is attacking two black pawns on e6 and g7, and the defensive 24...♛c5+ 25 ♔h2 (25 ♛d4!?) ♛e7 26 ♛d4 ♔b8 27 a4 is unclear: White's queen is excellently placed and he has attacking chances on the queenside. So Black played the crafty 24...♛c7! when White took the e-pawn: 25 ♛xe6+?. Instead, he should try 25 ♖e1 or 25 ♛d4, with only slightly worse chances. 25...♛d7!. Now the exchange of queens is forced, and despite White's extra pawn he has a lost position. His flimsy pawn structure cannot resist the attack of Black's rook and queen. The game concluded: 26 ♛xd7+ (26 ♛h3 ♛xh3 27 gxh3 ♖f3 is just as bad) 26...♔xd7 27 ♖b1 b6 28 ♖e1 ♔e6 29 a4 ♖f5 30 ♖e3 ♖xe5 31 ♔f2 (the pawn endgame is hopeless, but so is 31 ♖f3 ♖e1+ 32 ♔f2 ♖a1) 31...♖xe3 32 ♔xe3 h5 33 ♔f4 a5! (drawing back the white king with the threat of ...b7-b5) 34 ♔e3 ♔e5 35 ♔d2 ♔e4 36 ♔e2 d4 37 cxd4 ♔xd4 38 ♔d2 c3+ 39 ♔e2 ♔c4 40 ♔e3 ♔b4 41 ♔d3 ♔xa4 42 ♔xc3 ♔b5 43 ♔b3 ♔c5 0-1 (A.Nunez-McDonald, Andorra 1991)

10. White can draw with the simple 1 ♘e4 ♗xc3 (forced) 2 ♘xd6 ♗xe1 3 f3! intending 4 ♘e4 and 5 ♘xg5! leaving Black with the bishop and wrong rook's

pawn. But I wish to point out another draw: 1 ♗xf6 ♛xf6 2 ♘xh5! ♔xh5 3 ♖e3 with a blockade.

11. In the game Anand-J.Polgar, Linares 1994, the Indian grandmaster played 19 ♘xe6! fxe6 20 ♛xe6. The g6 pawn is now doomed so White acquires three strong pawns, which threaten to race up the board, for the piece. Black needs to use her extra piece to generate some compensating attacking chances against White's king. Unfortunately, the insecure position of her own king hampers her counterattack. 20...♔b8 (20...♗g7 21 ♗d4 ♗xd4 22 ♖xd4 leaves almost all Black's pawns hanging) 21 ♛xg6 ♖h3 22 ♔b1! (22 ♗d4 ♖xc3! 23 ♗xc3 ♛xa2 and 24...♘c5 gives Black good counterplay; White's game move avoids this counter-sacrifice since if 22...♖xc3 23 ♗e1! regains the material without creating a weakness) 22...♖f3 23 ♗d4 ♖xf4 24 ♛h7 (Black has broken up White's pawn phalanx but the g-pawn is now unstoppable except by sacrificing the f8 bishop, which will leave White a pawn up with a more compact position) 24...d5 (a desperate bid for activity) 25 g6 ♗c5 26 ♗xc5 ♘xc5 27 g7 (now the passed pawn will cost a rook) 27...♔a7 28 g8(♛) ♖xg8 29 ♛xg8 ♘xe4 30 ♘xe4 ♖xe4 31 ♛g7 ♛c5 32 ♖ge1 ♖f4 33 ♖e7 ♛b6 34 ♛g5 c3 35 b3

♕b4 36 ♖c7 ♖a4 37 ♕xd5 ♔b8 38 ♕d8+ ♔a7 39 a3 ♕xa3 and 1-0 before 40 ♖xc3.

12. The position occurred in Karpov-Yusupov, Tilburg 1993. White has a clear advantage and can even win the exchange immediately with 47 ♘xa7. However, the danger is that the position will become so blocked that White's rooks will be unable to penetrate into Black's position. So Karpov eschewed the win of the exchange and instead played **47 f6!**. This ensures that the f-file is opened, since if 47...♖b7 48 ♖f1 followed by 49 h7, 50 ♖h5 and 51 ♖xg5 will win. **47...♗xf6 48 ♖f1 ♗h8 49 ♘xa7** winning, but 49 ♖hf2 is simpler, e.g. 49...f6 50 h7 ♔f7 51 ♘xa7 ♖xa7 52 ♖xf6+ ♗xf6 53 h8(♕). **49...♖xa7 50 ♖h5** (still 50 ♖hf2 wins) **50...♔e7 51 ♖xg5 ♖a8 52 h7 f6 53 ♖g8 ♖f8 54 c5!** (this breakthrough method will by now be familiar to the reader) **54...dxc5 55 ♔c4 ♔f7 56 d6!** cxd6 57 ♖xf8+ ♔xf8 and **Black resigned** without waiting for the inevitable 58 ♔d5, 59 ♔c6 and 60 ♔xb6.

13. The author reached this position as Black against R.Wynarczyk at Whitby in 1991. I looked at 56...axb6 and saw it was only a draw after 57 axb6 ♗xb6 (57...♔f4 58 b7 ♗a7 59 ♔d3 is no better) 58 ♔d3 ♔f4 59 ♔e2 ♔g3 (if White's king

reaches h1 he draws, since Black has the wrong rook's pawn) 60 h4 ♔xh4 61 ♔f3 ♔h3 62 ♔f4 ♔h4 (White intended 63 g6! hxg6 64 ♔g5) 63 ♔f3 ♔h3 64 ♔f4 ♗d4 65 ♔f3 and I couldn't see a win (I still can't). So I played 56...a6. Then 57 h4 ♔f5 58 ♔d5 ♗xh4 59 ♔c6 ♗xg5 (59...♔xg5 60 ♔b7) 60 b7 ♗f4 61 ♔b6 ♔e6 (61...h5 62 ♔xa6 h4 63 ♔a7 h4 64 b8(♕) and the a-pawn reaches a7 after Black queens, with a draw) 62 ♔xa6 ♔d7 63 ♔a7 ♔c6 64 b8(♕) ♗xb8+ 65 ♔xb8 ♔b5. It seems as if White is lost, since his king is outside the 'square' of the h-pawn. But by making a feint to support the a-pawn, White snatches a draw: 66 ♔b7! ♔xa5 67 ♔c6 and a draw was agreed. After the game, Colin Crouch asked me why I did not play **56...♗xb6!**. It turns out to be more important to keep a queenside pawn than the bishop. Black wins by a tempo: **57 axb6 axb6 58 ♔b5 ♔f4 59 ♔xb6 ♔xg5 60 ♔c5 ♔h4 61 ♔d4 ♔xh3 62 ♔e3 ♔g3!** (62...♔g2 63 ♔f4) **63 ♔e2 ♔g2 64 ♔e3 h5 65 ♔f4 h4** and wins.

14. Apparently Black has a good game: a solid position, well developed pieces and a threat (22...♕xc2+). 22 ♘e7+ does not save White: 22...♖xe7 23 ♕xe7 ♕xc2+ 24 ♔a1 ♘c6! and White loses his queen because 25...♗xb2 mate is threatened. So White should cut his losses and

play **22 ♕xf8+ ♖xf8 23 ♘e7 mate** (Van Mil-Reinderman, Wijk aan Zee 1993). We repeat: tactics come before strategy. All generalised, verbal arguments cut no ice if it's mate in two. (White had just played the cunning 21 ♕d2-b4 and Black fell for it with 21...♕c6??.)

15. This position arose in the PCA Candidates match, Tiviakov-Adams, New York 1994. Rather than play 18 ♗xb4 with equal chances, White tried the enterprising **18 ♕xb7?!** sacrificing the exchange for a couple of pawns. **18...♘c2 19 ♖xa5** (19 ♗xa5 ♕d3 20 ♕xe7 ♕xb3 is good for Black) **19...♘xe1 20 ♖xa8 ♕xa8 21 ♕xa8** (of course 21 ♕xe7?? ♕xg2 is mate) **21...♖xa8 22 ♗xe1**. White's passed pawns look dangerous, but his pieces are loosely placed and until they can be redeployed, they cannot give the passed pawns much support. One of White's problems is that his other rook has been exchanged. Therefore Black's remaining rook has no rival. Adams exploited this in incisive style: **22...♖a4! 23 c5 ♖c4! 24 c6** (if the passed pawns were well supported, they would become more dangerous with every advance. Instead, they are targets for Black's pieces) **24...♘d5 25 ♘f1 ♔f8 26 ♘e3 ♘xe3 27 fxe3 ♔e8 28 ♗c3 ♗c5 29 ♔f2 ♗b6 30 ♔f3 ♔d8 31 ♗xg7** (White's passed pawns are stymied and the arrival of Black's

king is a portent of doom, so White surrenders the pawns to break up Black's kingside) **31...♖b4 32 ♘d4 ♗xd4 33 ♗xd4 ♖xb5 34 ♔e4 ♔c7 35 ♗c3 ♔xc6** and Black gradually exploited his material advantage to win on move 59.

16. **38 g4! gxh4** (or 38...hxg4 39 h5 ♔e6 40 fxg4 f5 - or else White plays his king to e4 and f5 - 41 h6 ♔f6 42 gxf5 and wins) **39 gxh5 ♔e6 40 ♔g2 ♔f5 41 f4!!** (the point) and **Black resigned** since 41...♔e6 42 ♔h3 wins.

17. Black has just played 22...♖d8-d7? which gave White the chance of a breakthrough on the kingside: **23 ♖xc8+ ♘xc8 24 f5! exf5 25 ♕h6**. Note that this penetration is only possible because Black's knight has been deflected from its role of defending the f5 square. **25...♖c7 26 ♖f2!**. The threat of ♘g5 hovers over Black and interferes with the coordination of his pieces. For example, 26...♘e7 27 ♘g5 would be decisive, since the rook on c7 no longer defends f7, so mate in two with 28 ♕h7+ is threatened (27...♘c6 28 e6!). Black's one chance is if he can gain counterplay against White's king with ...♕xd4 in reply to ♘g5. So White does not play ♘g5 but rather safeguards his king and prepares another breakthrough: e6. A good example of a threat being stronger than its execution. **26...a6**. Black

cannot see any way to improve his position. **27 ℤe2! ♕b5 28 ♔f2 ♕d3** (once again hoping for 29 ♘g5 ♕xd4+) **29 e6**. Now Black's kingside crumbles. **29...♘d6 30 exf7+ ℤxf7**. Of course, 30...♔xf7 31 ♘e5+ wins. **31 ♕xg6+ ℤg7 32 ♕xd6 h4 33 ♕d8+ ♔f7 34 ♘e5+ 1-0** (McDonald-Hastings, London 1993)

18. White played **27 d5! exd5** (if 27...ℤxd5 28 ♕e8+ wins). The sacrifice has a triple purpose, as soon becomes clear:
i) Open the e-file.
ii) Give the knight safe access to f5.
iii) Close the diagonal a8-h1.
You could hardly ask more from one move! Play concluded **28 ℤe8+ ℤxe8 29 ♕xe8+** (point i) **29...♗f8 30 ♘h6+ ♔g7 31 ♘f5+** (point ii) **31...♔g8 32 ℤa3!**. Point (iii)! The rook swings over and mates by 33 ℤg3+. If the a8-h1 diagonal were open, Black could counter with mate in three beginning 32...ℤc1+. (Los-Löffler, Amsterdam 1994)

19. Black has a lot of firepower directed against White's f3 pawn. One feels that a slight increase in the pressure will break down the defences. This is achieved with the sacrificial entrance of Black's bishop: **29...e5! 30 dxe5 ♗h3!** undermining the f-pawn's defender. White's position now collapses, since 31 ℤhg1 ♗xg2 and 32...ℤxf3+ is hopeless. **31**

gxh3 ℤxf3+ 32 ♕xf3 ℤxf3+ 33 ♔e2 ℤxh3 0-1 (Costa-Gavrikov, Switzerland 1994)

20. Black needs one more move for comfort: ...♗g7, adding another defender to the knight on f6. But it is White's move and he struck immediately with **22 c5!**. If the bishop were on g7, Black could now play 22...♘xc5 safely. But as things stand, both 22...♘xc5 and 22...dxc5 could be answered strongly by 23 fxe5. So Black can only accept the offer one way, and this leaves the queenside severely weakened: **22...bxc5 23 fxe5 dxe5 24 ♘c4** (a beautiful square for the knight, aiming both left, to a5, and tight, to e5) **24...♗g7** (the threat of 25 ♘4xe5 obliges Black to overprotect the knight on f6, but in doing so the square d6 is underprotected; White's next move exploits this fact to eventually win the exchange) **25 ♗c3!** (much better than the natural, obvious and inferior 25 ♘4xa5) **25...ℤe6** (defending against 26 ♗xa5 ♕b7 27 ♘d6, but now disaster strikes on a different square) **26 ♗xa5 ♕b7 27 ♘d8 ℤxd8 28 ♗xd8 ♕xb5 29 ♕d3 h5 30 ℤb1 ♕a6 31 ℤfe1 h4** (Black battles on, but the material deficit is fatal) **32 ℤb3 ♕c6 33 ♗xf6 ♘xf6 34 ℤb6 ♕c8 35 ℤxe6 ♕xe6 36 a4 ♗h6 37 a5 ♘h5 38 ♕d5 ♕g4 39 ♕xf7! ♔h8 40 ♘xe5 ♘f4 41 ♕xf4 1-0** (Ftacnik-Gedevanishvili, Sydney 1991).